THE
POWER
OF
GOD'S WORD

FOR
HEALING

VOLUME 1

VITAL KEYS
TO VICTORY OVER SICKNESS

BY ANNE B. BUCHANAN

The Power of God's Word for Healing: Vital Keys to Victory Over Sickness   (Christian Devotional Healing Series, Volume 1)
Copyright © 2011, 2014, 2018 by Anne B. Buchanan

Previously published under the title *Healing in His Wings* © 2000 Anne B. Buchanan. Now updated, revised, and divided into four volumes under the title, *The Power of God's Word*.

Unless otherwise indicated, all Scripture quotations are taken from the *King James Version* (KJV) of the Bible.

Scripture quotations marked (AMP) are taken from The Amplified Bible. Scripture taken from THE AMPLIFIED BIBLE, Old Testament copyright © 1965, 1987 by the Zondervan Corporation. The Amplified New Testament copyright © 1958, 1987 by The Lockman Foundation. Used by permission.

Printed in the United States of America

Disclaimer / Limitations of Liability

All material in this book is for information and educational purposes only. No information concerning matters of health is intended as a means to diagnose or treat diseases. No information is intended to be a substitute for medical advice by a licensed health care provider. All readers should consult a licensed health care provider and The Great Physician in all matters relating to medical problems, especially in matters of diagnosing or treating diseases or other physical and mental conditions. The Author and Publisher do not directly or indirectly give medical advice, nor do they prescribe any supplements or assume any responsibility or liability for those who treat themselves. No statements in this publication have been analyzed or approved by the FDA.

Dedicated

To The Glory of God
Who Loves Us
And Who Heals Us

In Memory of
My mother, Elizabeth

TABLE OF CONTENTS

Preface 13

Day 1
God's Plan For Your Health 17

Day 2
Jesus Took Your Sicknesses 19

Day 3
Speak To Your Mountain 21

Day 4
By His Stripes You Were Healed 23

Day 5
Jesus Healed Them All 25

Day 6
Jesus Followed Father God's Instructions 27

Day 7
What Does "Sozo" Mean? 31

Day 8
The Devil Comes To Steal, Kill, and Destroy 33

Day 9
You Determine Your Life With Your Words 35

Day 10
Your Faith Is Substance 37

Day 11
The Power of the Words "I AM" 39

Day 12
You Have Authority Over the Enemy 41

Day 13
Your Words Either Empower or Bind Satan 43

Day 14
God's Will Be Done On Earth 45

Day 15
You Can Have the Petitions You Ask 47

Day 16
Thank God In Advance 51

Day 17
The Power Of A Prayer Of Agreement 53

Day 18
Speak What You Want 55

Day 19
Seek God's Way For Your Healing 59

Day 20
Herbs Are God's Remedies for Healing 61

Day 21
It Is Written 63

Day 22
Fear Not 65

Day 23
Emotional Healing 67

Day 24
God's Benefits 69

Day 25
The Word of God Is Life 71

Day 26
Your Body Is the Temple of the Holy Spirit 75

Day 27
Resist the Devil 77

Day 28
Your Emotions Affect Your Physical Health 79

Day 29
Your Body Hears What You Say 81

Day 30
Will You Be Made Whole? 83

Day 31
Disciples Are to Heal, Deliver, and Preach 85

Day 32
You Are Surrounded By Heavenly Help 87

Day 33
It Is Finished 89

Day 34
God Does Not Lie 91

Day 35
Prosper and Be in Health 93

Day 36
Believe You Have What You Say 95

Day 37
How to Pray 97

Day 38
The Power That Works in You 99

Day 39
God Gives Good Gifts 101

Day 40
Use the Faith You Have 103

Day 41
The Measure of Faith 105

Day 42
The Light of God's Word 107

Day 43
The Power of Giving Thanks 109

Day 44
Jesus Is Your Secure Rock 111

Day 45
The Peace of God 113

Day 46
Do All Things Work for Your Good? 115

Day 47
The Holy Spirit Teaches You 117

Day 48
Does Healing Surprise You? 119

Day 49
The Problem of Unbelief 121

Day 50
Root Out Unbelief 123

Day 51
Don't Be Divided Against Yourself 125

Day 52
Can You Really Do Greater Things Than Jesus? 127

Day 53
Don't Give Up! 129

Day 54
Rise and Walk in the Name of Jesus 131

Day 55
Be Careful What You Think 133

Day 56
Hope Means Expectation 135

Day 57
Keep Scriptures in Front of You 137

Day 58
What Do You Want from Jesus? 139

Day 59
Choose Life 141

Day 60
Be Restored 143

Day 61
You Are As You Think in Your Heart 145

Day 62
The Blessing of Communion 147

Day 63
Be Made Whole 149

Day 64
Power Over All the Power of the Enemy 153

Day 65
The Bible Is God's Inspired Word 155

Day 66
Jesus and the Father Are One 157

Day 67
God Keeps His Covenant 161

Day 68
Jesus Healed Them All 163

Day 69
Freely Give What You Have Received 165

Day 70
Arise and Walk in Victory 167

Great Resources

Our YouTube Channel 169

Books and Teaching CDs 169

Music – Online, Downloads, CDs 173

Audiobooks 173

Books by Anne B. Buchanan 174

A Final Word 176

✝
PREFACE

"If God is a healer, then why am I sick?" This question used to bother me a lot. Some people got well. Some people died. And some people like me eventually were learning to "live with" and "manage" their ailments. Deep in my heart, I just could not accept that it was God's will to heal some people and not others – especially when I seemed to be in the "not others" category.

Step-by-step God began to show me how I had misunderstood His Word, and He began to reveal His truths about healing. It is my joy to share what I have learned with you in this first volume of *The Power of God's Word* series.

One of the major turning points for me came when I learned the meaning of the Greek word "*sozo*," which is translated "save" in English. Because I did not know the Greek language, I always missed the full impact of what the Holy Spirit was saying in numerous Scriptures. Once I was introduced to the *Strong's Concordance* and I could examine any word in the Bible, an entirely new level of revelation opened up to me.

The Greek word "*sozo*" means "to save, heal, deliver, and make whole." Therefore, it expresses far more than the

English translation, "save," conveys. I went through the New Testament and searched for every place where I saw the word "save." I looked in my concordance to see if the Greek word was "sozo," and, if so, I wrote the full meaning of the word in the margin of my Bible. When I re-read the passage of Scripture using the full meaning, I was astonished at the message that God was telling me.

I am sharing that revelation with you in this book and hope that it will be as uplifting and illuminating for you as it has been for me. In this book you will learn about God's healing power and how to be made whole through the precious blood of Jesus. It is all about learning what Jesus *really* did for us on the Cross and how to exercise the authority He won for us.

In my own personal life, I find that God's Word and God's remedies make a powerful combination for healing. The God who created me also created the plants, herbs, and essential oils, and I believe He did so with full *intention* – knowing exactly how my body works and how these natural substances meet my bodily needs. However, I want to emphasize that I never forget that it is the Creator who is to be exalted, not the creation. It is the Lord God Almighty who is my Healer, rather than any substance which I may use temporarily to assist my bodily functions to return to a proper balance.

Each person has to take full responsibility for his own health and make his own personal decision about medical care. Those who are on medications need to be particularly cautious. Some medications create a serious physical dependency in the natural world and to discontinue them suddenly can lead to rapid death unless God intervenes supernaturally. God's Word tells us we are not to tempt Him.

Therefore, to discontinue any medication in a rush of "instant faith" would most likely be a fatal decision that would delight the evil one. Don't do it. Instead, strengthen your faith, pray with your medical counselors, and seek God's instruction and your doctor's instructions about what changes to make and when to make them. I am not a medical doctor and do not prescribe or suggest any medical treatments. Please heed the disclaimer in this book and seek appropriate health care professionals in matters concerning your health.

Please note that I have occasionally taken a few liberties with the English language in this book. I have bent a few rules of grammar so that what you read matches the way that people speak. I have also intentionally spelled satan's name with a small "s" except at the beginning of a sentence. Writing his name in lower case provides a visual reminder that he has been totally defeated by our Risen Savior and has only the power we choose to give him.

This book proclaims God's healing power in small daily doses, boosting our faith step by step and reminding us of God's Holy Word and His covenant with us. It is easy to talk about faith and quite another to navigate the path of healing with focus and purpose. I hope that all who read these messages will be blessed by them.

At the end of the book are a few selected references to materials which you may find useful if you wish to explore further. I am very grateful for those who have long proclaimed God's healing message and who have been instrumental in helping me along the way.

If you like this volume of *The Power of God's Word*, please take a look at the other volumes in the series, which are available from Amazon .com in paperback and on Kindle. Audiobooks are available from Amazon.com, iTunes.com, and Audible.com.

We also have a YouTube channel called Proclaiming God's Word, which has uplifting, encouraging, and peaceful videos on topics such as Scriptures for healing, Scriptures for sleep, and Scriptures for overcoming depression. Please take a look at them at:

http://YouTube.com/c/ProclaimingGodsWord.

Many blessings to each one of you,

Anne Buchanan

P.S. If you like this book, it would be a great blessing to me if you would go to Amazon.com and leave a review in the "Customer Reviews" section. Thank you.

†

DAY 1
GOD'S PLAN FOR YOUR HEALTH

... I am the Lord that healeth thee.   (Exodus 15:26)

It's time to discover what you've missed.   Are you struggling with cancer or allergies or depression? Have you been praying for healing and relief – but you're still sick? Let today be a fresh start on an exciting journey as step by step God speaks directly to you through His Word. He loves you and He wants you well. If you're sick, find out the reason why.

Begin with this glorious declaration of the Lord God Almighty, "I am the Lord who heals you." Our God is the God of healing, and He offers you His Word to seal His covenant.

It's crucial to believe deep within your heart that God wants you to be healthy. You may have believed that illness is a part of God's plan for His children. Or you may have believed that you are being punished for some past wrongdoing. Or you may have believed that you are being taught a lesson. Whatever your thoughts may have been, read God's Word now with new eyes. Open your mind and your heart to receive new revelation of God's will for you.

When God first created His beloved children, He placed Adam and Eve in a wondrous garden where only goodness surrounded them. Sickness and disease didn't exist. In the garden we see the perfect expression of God's will. He wanted us to walk with Him and commune with Him in the fullness and abundance of life.

Did God's will change? Of course not. Man's will changed. Man's will shifted from obedience to disobedience to eat of the fruit and know evil when Eve believed a lie from the devil and Adam joined her in disobeying God's instructions. Sickness and disease occurred only when Adam and Eve chose to include evil in their world. That was a result of their will, not God's. God's will never changes, and His will is for you to be healthy.

No matter what your past has been, God wants you to be well so that you can live an abundant, vibrant life in service to Him. He has declared Himself as the God who heals you. Today allow your Heavenly Father to share His heart with you through His covenant promises, His Word, and revelation of the Holy Spirit. Receive His love and His healing grace.

Father God, today I'm starting over. I've been struggling for too long and I'm tired of it. Your Word says that You are the God who heals me. Well, I've been praying for my healing and it hasn't manifested yet. I'm ready to learn, to know what has stood in the way of my recovery, and to make changes in my life. I've decided to look with new eyes at Your Holy Word, so show me, Father, what I've missed. In Jesus' name, I pray, Amen.

✝

DAY 2
JESUS TOOK YOUR SICKNESSES

... and he cast out the spirits with his word, and healed all that were sick: That it might be fulfilled which was spoken by Esaias the prophet, saying, "Himself took our infirmities and bare our sicknesses." (Matthew 8:16-17)

Jesus Christ came for one purpose – to redeem us. God wanted His children to be restored and made whole according to His original plan. Give yourself permission to believe that this redemption was not just of our spirits and our souls but also of our *bodies* as well.

Most people think that the atonement of the Cross provided only for our spiritual redemption. It's certainly true that the blood of Jesus atoned for our sins. Hebrews 9:26 says, "... but now once in the end of the world hath he appeared to put away sin by the sacrifice of himself."

But look again at Matthew 8:16-17. Matthew tells us that the atonement includes the healing of our bodies as well. Notice that the Scripture uses the past tense to describe the finished work of Jesus. Jesus *took* our infirmities. Jesus *bore* our sicknesses. It is done, finished, completed. Jesus took every curse upon Himself and broke them forever. He redeemed us spiritually from our sins, our past, our patterns, and our mistakes. In addition, Matthew makes it very clear that Jesus also bore our physical sicknesses and infirmities.

Just think of that. Jesus bore your sickness. He died to redeem you, soul and *body*. Let that incredible truth sink into every cell of your body. See Jesus on the Cross carrying not only your sins but also your sicknesses. Name each one of your ailments, and one by one give them all to Jesus on the Cross. Acknowledge the awesome truth that Jesus overcame them all. He died for *you*.

Now open your heart to your Risen Lord and accept His healing power in your body. Say to yourself, "Jesus took *my* infirmities and bore *my* sicknesses. In the name of Jesus I am healed." Repeat this healing truth many times during the day knowing that God's Word is true.

Jesus has already redeemed you, every part of you. His atonement is finished and complete. Everything has been done by your loving Savior. All you have to do is believe and receive the healing of the Resurrection.

Almighty Father, thank You for loving me so much that You sent Your Son, Jesus Christ, to save, redeem, and heal me. I lay each of my ailments at the foot of Calvary's Cross, and I believe Your Holy Word which declares that Jesus bore not only my sins but also my sicknesses. I accept my healing, and I receive it now in the name of my Savior, Christ Jesus. In gratitude and praise I pray, Amen.

†

DAY 3
SPEAK TO YOUR MOUNTAIN

... for verily I say unto you, If ye have faith as a grain of mustard seed, ye shall say unto this mountain, Remove hence to yonder place; and it shall remove; and nothing shall be impossible unto you. (Matthew 17:20)

Here Jesus gives you the key to your healing, which is to believe in God's will for your healing and then speak your belief forcefully. Trust and have faith, remembering that the *size* of your faith is not the issue. You need to have only as much faith as a tiny grain of mustard seed. What is relevant, however, is the *quality* of your faith. It must be focused, concentrated, and whole. Each mustard seed is tiny, yet it is as whole as a large avocado pit.

Nothing is impossible to you. Nothing. No matter what. No matter how many medical opinions you may have received. No matter how many tests show your problems "in black and white." No matter how many symptoms you see and feel manifested in your body. No matter how big the mountain is, nothing shall be impossible unto you if you have a concentrated, tiny nugget of faith, trust, and belief.

Remember that "faith without works is dead" (James 2:20). It is critically important to act on your faith

21

because by doing so, you take authority over the enemy and boldly reinforce the power of God's Word in your life.

Therefore, here in Matthew, Jesus tells you to confront the problem by looking directly at your mountain and then speaking the outcome that you desire. You must *say* to the mountain, "Remove hence to yonder place." Words of faith are simple, few, and to the point, allowing God's will to be fulfilled in your life.

Speak to your physical ailment now. For example, say, "Heart disease, remove yourself from my body now in the name of Jesus." Or say, "Tumors, I command that you disappear now in Jesus' name."

Focus on God's Word. Focus on your Savior, Jesus Christ, who died for your healing as He also died for your sins. Focus on the truth that nothing is impossible to those who believe and declare their faith boldly to the Lord God Almighty.

Father God, it is written that nothing is impossible if I have faith. I declare my trust in You and I declare my faith in You. I hold tightly to my mustard seed faith and speak it boldly. Although my physical eyes may see the mountain of illness before me, I stand on Your Holy Word and say to all my illnesses, "Remove hence!" I choose to see with my spiritual eyes that every organ in my body is strong and healthy. And so it is according to Your Word and Your Son, Christ Jesus, in whose name I pray, Amen.

†

DAY 4
BY HIS STRIPES YOU WERE HEALED

Who his own self bare our sins in his own body on the tree, that we, being dead to sins, should live unto righteousness: by whose stripes ye were healed. (1 Peter 2:24)

This is one of the most familiar Scriptures in the Bible, yet many of us have never really understood what it is saying. "By His stripes you were healed." Here is the past tense again. You *were* healed. How can that be true?

If you examine the Word, you see again and again an emphasis on the finished work of the Cross. This Scripture plainly says that through the wounds, stripes, and beatings that Jesus took in our place, He paid for our healing. He paid the price once and for all. It is finished. Yet we still often beg and plead, "Oh, God, please heal me. Will you please heal me? Please do something." Do you see that such a prayer is asking God to give you what He has already accomplished through the beatings and crucifixion of Jesus?

Imagine for a moment that horrendous day when Jesus stood before Pilate with His arms bound. Barabbas was released and "then Pilate therefore took Jesus, and scourged [whipped] him" (John 19:1). "And they spit upon him, and took the reed, and smote him on the head" (Matthew 27:30).

Make the words in those two verses come alive in your mind so that you can comprehend that redemption was not

23

just a spiritual event. See each blow fall on Jesus' body. Feel each blow as it lands. Jesus bore the assaults on His physical body because He was taking them for you. For *you*.

Blow after blow fell on Him and ripped His flesh open. Why? Because "by His stripes we were healed." Jesus paid every price so that you would be made perfectly whole. With each blow *you* are healed. Lay an ailment at the feet of Jesus. Wham! Jesus has overcome it. Lay another health condition at His feet. Wham! Jesus has overcome it. And another and another and another. Jesus has overcome them all.

By His stripes your healing was provided for you. Rejoice! Believe God's Word and receive your healing now.

Heavenly Father, I come with tears in my eyes for the overwhelming sacrifice of Your Son, Jesus Christ, who died for my sins. Mine. And who bore my infirmities on the Cross. Mine. I can barely comprehend this magnificent gift of salvation and redemption. It is written that by the stripes of Your Son, Jesus Christ, I was healed. I stand on Your Holy Word as every part of my body recovers to perfect health. With a heart filled with faith, praise, and gratitude, I pray in Jesus' name, Amen.

†

DAY 5
JESUS HEALED THEM ALL

And Jesus went about all Galilee, teaching in their synagogues, and preaching the gospel of the kingdom, and healing all manner of sickness and all manner of disease among the people.

And his fame went throughout all Syria: and they brought unto him all sick people that were taken with divers diseases and torments, and those which were possessed with devils, and those which were lunatic, and those that had the palsy; and he healed them. (Matthew 4:23-24)

Notice how often the word "all" appears in the Gospels to describe those whom Jesus healed. This tiny, easily overlooked word reinforces the limitless power of God. In this passage in Matthew we find Jesus going throughout all Galilee. And what was He doing? Two things. First, He was telling people His message by teaching and preaching, and second, He was healing the sick.

What kinds of sicknesses did the people have who came to Him? "All manner of sickness." "All manner of disease." Those with "divers [various] diseases and torments." "Those which were possessed with devils and those which were lunatic." "Those that had the palsy." The list does not leave out any kind of illness or disease whatsoever. ALL manner of disease, birth defects, and mental illness.

Is there any health problem at the physical or mental level that would not have been covered by this Scripture? If you had been in Galilee, would your illness have "qualified" you to be in the crowd of the sick as described by Matthew? The answer has to be yes. No illness was beyond the healing power of Jesus.

Who of the sick people was He healing? ALL of those who wanted healing and who came to Him. The Scripture says, "... he healed them" – period. If you had been in Galilee and you sought Jesus, you would have been healed because Matthew's description excludes no one. Jesus excluded no one. He reached out to touch every one who came to Him to be made well. Every single one.

Do you believe Jesus *could* have healed you in Galilee? Do you believe Jesus *would* have healed you in Galilee? If you do, then receive His healing that has been made available to every believer through the shed blood of the Cross.

Father God, when Your Son walked on earth, He always acted according to Your will and He healed everybody who came to Him of whatever kind of sickness they had. There was no illness beyond His power. I come before You today and stand in total faith. I rejoice in knowing that Jesus has paid the price for my physical healing, and I declare, according to Your Holy Word, that by His stripes I was – and am – healed. In Jesus' name, I pray, Amen.

✝

Day 6
Jesus Followed
Father God's Instructions

But [Satan is coming and] I do as the Father has commanded Me, so that the world may know (be convinced) that I love the Father and that I do only what the Father has instructed Me to do. [I act in full agreement with His orders.] (John 14:31 Amplified Bible)

Jesus tells us that every single thing that He does carries out an instruction of God the Father. "I love the Father and ... do *only* what the Father has instructed Me to do."

The Amplified Bible explains that Jesus is "acting in full agreement with God's orders." What a marvelous way to express that verse! Father God gave all the orders, and Jesus put Himself in full agreement with (and perfect submission to) those orders. He didn't just hear the orders, but He acted on them to carry them out completely and perfectly. Holy Scripture is clear that Jesus operated under the direct authority of Father God and always manifested His perfect will.

Because Jesus always fulfilled God the Father's will, satan tried to attack Him, but he never succeeded. Jesus warned that satan was on the attack. The devil even tried to have Jesus stoned (John 8:59 and John 10:31) but none of his attacks succeeded because they couldn't penetrate the authority of Jesus.

Please note that there is no record of Jesus' ever being sick. He suffered every trial and tribulation that we do except illness. Just as Jesus was without sin while He was here on earth, He was also without sickness. It was only on the Cross that Jesus became both sin and sickness for us.

Be clear in your mind and heart that Jesus did *only* the will of the Father. Also be clear in your mind and heart that Jesus did *only* those things which He was commanded and instructed to do. Now consider the fact that Jesus healed *everyone* who asked for healing. Holy Scripture says it over and over and over again. He healed them *all*.

Jesus never told anyone that God wanted that person to remain sick. He never told anyone that God was trying to teach him a lesson through his illness. He never refused to heal anyone, not ever. It was only in Nazareth, where the people did not believe Him, that He was unsuccessful in healing.

Now you must decide if you believe that Jesus' actions were only for the people of Galilee two thousand years ago, or if they apply to you right now in the twenty-first century. Jesus knew His mission of salvation was to heal the hearts and bodies of God's beloved children. Through Him our sins are washed away and with His stripes we are healed. Open your heart and let the Holy Spirit reveal God's truth to you.

Father God, Your Word says that everything Jesus did was according to Your will, Your instruction, and Your commandment. I join You, Father, in full agreement with Your Word, and I will not pick and choose what part I want to believe and enforce. You provided the complete package through Jesus – salvation, healing, deliverance, and being made whole. I have received Jesus Christ into my heart, and, therefore, I receive His healing now as Your will for me. Help me to follow the instructions of the Holy Spirit so that I can be the witness for You that You want me to be. I thank You and I give You all the praise and all the glory. In the name of Jesus Christ, I pray, Amen.

✝

DAY 7
WHAT DOES "SOZO" MEAN?

And Jesus said unto him, Receive thy sight: thy faith hath saved thee. (Luke 18:42)

And the prayer of faith shall save the sick, and the Lord shall raise him up. (James 5:15)

For by grace are ye saved through faith; and that not of yourselves: it is the gift of God. (Ephesians 2:8)

We find the English word "save" in each of these three verses. When we speak of being "saved," we think of giving our heart to Jesus, of having our sins forgiven, and of being assured of spending eternity in heaven with God. But how does the word "save" fit with the first two passages which are clearly talking about healing of the body?

For that answer we have to go back to the original Greek language of the New Testament. The English word "save" was translated from the Greek word "*sozo*," which is a verb that means save, deliver, protect, heal, and make whole. Notice that being saved and being healed are bound together in the meaning of the word just as Jesus repeatedly bound them together in His description of His mission and purpose.

Now let's expand on the verse in Luke using the full meaning of the Greek word "*sozo*." Jesus said to the blind

31

man, "Receive your sight. Your faith has healed, saved, delivered, and made you whole." Awesome, isn't it? And the verse in James becomes "and the prayer of faith shall heal, save, deliver, and make whole those who are sick." Wow!

Lastly, Paul writes that "by grace are you saved, healed, delivered, and made whole through faith, and that not of yourselves because it is the gift of God." What richness this understanding brings to the Word of God!

Check every Scripture where you see the word "save" in English. See if the Greek word is "sozo" or one of its related words. If so, write the full meaning of the word in the margin of your Bible and say all the words included in the Greek meaning each time you read that verse. Embrace the full meaning of being made whole through your faith in Jesus Christ and in His finished work of the Cross.

Father God, I did not realize what the Greek word "sozo" means, so all the passages of Your Word where that word is used are coming alive for me now. I understand that I am saved, healed, delivered, and made whole through the shed blood of Jesus. I stand in faith and receive my healing. In Jesus' name, I pray, Amen.

†

Day 8
The Devil Comes
To Steal, Kill, and Destroy

The thief cometh not, but for to steal, and to kill, and to destroy: I am come that they might have life, and that they might have it more abundantly. (John 10:10)

Jesus tells us what the devil is trying to do to us. He steals, kills, and destroys. His tool is deception, and he sends symptoms of disease.

Jesus Himself told us that satan was the source of illness in Luke 13:16. He said that the woman who was bent over with an extreme back curvature had been bound by satan for eighteen years. Jesus did not say that God had some purpose for the woman's deformity. He did not say it was a blessing. He did not say it was a lesson from God. He said the attack came from the devil, and He healed the woman immediately to set her free.

It is really imperative for you to decide who the source of sickness is. Is God blessing you with sickness? Or is the devil cursing you with illness? Your answer will determine your response. You can never fight satan effectively if you're not sure whether he is your enemy. Instead, you will be passive and accepting of whatever outcome happens. If you think God is the source of your illness, then satan is off the hook and totally out of the picture.

Think about this logically. If God made you sick and it is His will for you to be ill, then you should accept His will completely. Going to the doctor and getting treatment would be direct rebellion against God's will for you. In fact, maybe you should want two cancers instead of one to get a double blessing or a double lesson. That is, of course, ridiculous, but all the time we proclaim that our illness is God's will, we never stop to think that, if that is true, we have no right to interfere with God's plan.

God does *not* want you to be sick. It is the enemy who comes to steal your health and money and time. It is the enemy who wants to kill you. And it is the enemy who wants to destroy your life and your joy.

How wonderful it is to proclaim that Jesus is our Risen Lord who has won joyous, abundant life for us!

Father God, I know that my health problem didn't come from You. I submit myself to You totally, Lord. You tell me clearly that it is the enemy who comes to steal my health, kill my body, and destroy my happiness. I make a decision now to line up everything I say with Your Word. How wonderful it is to proclaim that by the stripes of Jesus I am healed. I receive the manifestation of total health now. In the glorious name of Jesus Christ, my Savior and my Redeemer, I pray, Amen.

†

DAY 9
YOU DETERMINE YOUR LIFE
WITH YOUR WORDS

Thou shalt also decree a thing, and it shall be established unto thee. (Job 22:28)

What staggering authority your words have! God plainly tells you that He allows you to determine your life through the words that you speak. He allows your free will to establish what happens to you. God creates with His Word, and He has established that you do the same.

Remember the situation described in the Book of Numbers when the Israelites were grumbling to Moses and Aaron, saying, "Would God that we had died in the land of Egypt! Or would God we had died in this wilderness!" (Numbers 14:2). Even though they had witnessed miraculous signs both in Egypt and in the desert, they loudly proclaimed all the details of their problems. Their words revealed their lack of faith that God would keep His Word and would deliver them to the home He had promised. This angered God and He said to them, "As you have spoken in my ears, so will I do to you" (Numbers 14:28).

We are no longer subject to judgment similar to that of the Israelites because Jesus took God's punishment in our place when He died on the Cross. However, the principle that we create with our words is still true. When we speak words that agree with God's Word, we can be assured that they will be fulfilled because God's Word never returns to Him void (Isaiah 55:11). However, when we speak words that do not agree with God's Word, the enemy is quick to use them against us.

Do you repeatedly say to everyone, "I'm a heart patient"? If so, you have decreed that you are a heart patient and you have invited the enemy to increase his attacks on your body. Or do you say, "I've been praying, but I'm just not getting any better"? If so, you have decreed that you are not getting any better, and the enemy is delighted to steal your recovery.

Each one of these "ordinary" statements betrays a lack of faith that the victory over your illness has already been won by Jesus Christ. Each one hinders God's blessing from coming to you and opens the door to the enemy. Guard the words you speak, and make sure they are ones that you want to be manifested in your life.

Almighty God, I haven't understood that You have given me the power to decree those things that will be established in my life. From this moment on, Lord, I won't pray about the problems that I see, but I will pray and speak only those things that are in agreement with Your Word. I will declare the end result that I desire and will stand firm in my faith until my healing is fully manifested. In Jesus' name, I pray, Amen.

†

DAY 10
YOUR FAITH IS SUBSTANCE

Now faith is the substance of things hoped for, the evidence of things not seen. (Hebrews 11:1)

We like to say, "Seeing is believing." However, Father God is a spirit, and His truth, the *real* truth, is just the reverse – believing is seeing. God asks you to believe *before* you see. It takes no faith at all to believe for something that you already see or possess. It is only when you *can't* see something that faith is required.

When you feel ill, your symptoms parade before you and scream at you. They are real. However, God encourages you over and over again in His Word to remember that there is a spiritual reality that is more important than the physical reality. God's truth points you to a different reality *beyond* your symptoms and *beyond* your illness. You must grasp at the core of your being that your ailments have their source in the father of lies. The evil one wants you to focus on the appearance of your situation and buy into it.

This is the time to exercise your faith. What is faith? It is *substance*, something that is also very real. It is *evidence*, but only of what cannot be seen. This is a very difficult concept for us to grasp because we live in a world of machines that can see into our bodies, and we are bombarded by tests that produce official-looking reports.

37

Yes, all these things exist. Yes, they are facts. Yes, they are real.

However, remember that the conclusions that are drawn from them are based entirely on elements from the physical realm. God's Word tells us that there is another dimension beyond the physical. It is substantial and it is evidence. Evidence of what? Of the things that are unseen.

All of the most important things of life are unseen. The Lord God Almighty Himself is unseen. Science will never find Him under a microscope or with a test of any kind. Love is unseen. Science will never find it with an MRI scan or in a blood test. The Holy Spirit is unseen. Science will never find Him with surgery or EKGs or ultrasound.

Believe in God's Holy Word. Hide in your heart God's truth that the most powerful evidence of all is unseen by the external eye. Exercise your faith by looking with your spiritual eyes at God's promises to you.

Father God, teach me to focus on Your truth and believe with all my heart that my healing is already real in the spiritual realm through the atonement of the Cross. I look with eyes of faith beyond the symptoms that I see and beyond the conclusions drawn from medical tests. I stand on Your Word which says that the real evidence is my healing which has already been won for me on the Cross. In Jesus' name, I pray, Amen.

†

DAY 11
THE POWER OF THE WORDS "I AM"

Jesus saith unto him, "I am the way, the truth, and the life."
(John 14:6)

When Moses wanted to know what name to use for God, God told him, "I AM who I AM" (which is "Yahweh" in Hebrew and "Jehovah" in English). God is the great "I AM," and He gave special importance to those words and whatever descriptions followed them.

As the Son of God, Jesus also knew of the importance of "I am." He knew that, when we use those words, we define ourselves. Watch how Jesus defines Himself. "I am the bread of life." "I am the light of the world." "I am the good shepherd." "I am the resurrection and the life." "I am the true vine." "I am the way, the truth, and the life."

What about you? Do you often define yourself by your illnesses or state of health? Do you say, "I am anemic" or "I am a diabetic" or "I am sick"? None of these definitions of yourself as a sick person describe who you are in God's eyes. Like all words we speak, each of these statements has power, and our soul and body take in the words and believe them.

We perpetuate and live our definitions of ourselves at every level of our being. When we define ourselves by our ailments, satan is delighted. He gains great power when we become so enmeshed with our illnesses that we no longer see ourselves whole and healthy. Our very language keeps us bound to our diseases.

Now you have an opportunity to speak God's truth instead of satan's deceptions. Notice how often you use "I am" followed by some indication of poor health, and then change what you are saying. For example, use "I feel" instead of "I am" by saying, "I feel sick" or "I feel tired." Better yet say, "I am being attacked with flu symptoms at the moment, but I stand on God's Word that 'by His stripes I am healed.'" By describing health conditions as something you are experiencing temporarily at the present time, you re-enforce God's truth that you are healed through the stripes of Jesus.

As you use the powerful words "I am" in ways that reflect God's will and God's vision for you, you will become more and more confident in God's promises. And you will see your faith strengthen and grow.

Dear Heavenly Father, help me to choose my words with care. Let not only the meditations of my heart but also the words of my mouth declare Your vision of me. I make a new commitment today to honor and respect the words "I am" and to change my pattern of speech so that what I say about myself lines up with what the Word says. You see me as healed through the blood of Jesus so I declare now that I am healed. In Jesus' name, I pray, Amen.

†

DAY 12
YOU HAVE AUTHORITY OVER THE ENEMY

Behold, I give unto you power to tread on serpents and scorpions, and over all the power of the enemy: and nothing shall by any means hurt you.

Notwithstanding in this rejoice not, that the spirits are subject unto you; but rather rejoice, because your names are written in heaven. (Luke 10:19-20)

Many Christians do not like to talk about the devil or even think about him. They don't want to give him any power so they believe that by ignoring him, they can make him go away and leave them alone. To support this position, they attribute many works of the enemy to God instead. They passively accept as blessings in disguise or as tribulations to be endured many of the items clearly described as curses in Deuteronomy 28:15-61.

Jesus never shared that view. He, and all the writers of the New Testament, readily acknowledged the presence and destructive activity of satan. Until Jesus came, people had no weapons against the devil that were effective and certain of victory. One of the things that separates us as Christians from all other religions is that through the name of Jesus we have authority over the devil and the entire demonic kingdom. It is the name and blood of Jesus and *only* the name and blood of Jesus that gives us this authority.

41

Colossians 2:15 says that the Lord "having spoiled principalities and powers, made a show of them openly, triumphing over them in it." Because Jesus defeated satan, He has the power to delegate His authority to us.

Notice that Jesus *expected* the spirits to obey and, therefore, He warned His followers not to put any emphasis on this delegated power but to stay focused on the most important thing which was that their destination was to live with God for all eternity.

Engrave Luke 10:19 into your heart. It is one of the most powerful weapons in your arsenal. If the enemy attacks you with some symptom, take your authority and say, "No! Spirits of infirmity, I enforce Luke 10:19 on you. It is written that I have power over all the power of the enemy so, Pain, I command you to leave my body now in the name of Jesus."

Speak the words of Luke 10:19 and command tumors to leave, legs to stand, and itching to stop. See every lying symptom as a snake coming toward you and trample it beneath your feet in the name of your Lord and Savior.

Father God, I take the authority given to me by Your Son to trample on the enemy and to command him to leave in the mighty name of Jesus. I thank You for this power, Father, but I rejoice not that the evil spirits are subject to me but that my name is written in heaven. In Jesus' name, I pray, Amen.

✝

DAY 13
YOUR WORDS
EITHER EMPOWER OR BIND SATAN

And I will give unto thee the keys of the kingdom of heaven: and whatsoever thou shalt bind on earth shall be bound in heaven: and whatsoever thou shalt loose on earth shall be loosed in heaven.
(Matthew 16:19)

Many people skip past this statement of Jesus, even though it is so important that it appears in Scripture twice. In fact, Jesus tells us what He is saying is so vital that He considers it to be *the keys of the kingdom of heaven.* "Whatsoever you bind on earth will be bound in heaven, and whatsoever you loose on earth will be loosed in heaven." One more time we are told that our lives are largely the result of our own free will and not God's will. When our lives are going well, we like to take credit for our hard work. But when difficulties come, Christians are quick to point the finger at God and say that it is "God's will."

Jesus reminds us that God gave us dominion over the earth and that He gave us free will. He tells us that we must take responsibility not only for our actions but also for our words. When we feel sick, we can either bind the enemy from his attacks on us or we can hinder our ability to receive the healing power of God that has already been released for us. We can either loose the power of God's

Word in our lives or we can loose further attacks of satan. The choice is ours.

We do it primarily by our words. If you say, "I feel terrible and I'm getting worse," then you hinder God's power because it is written that we are to speak to our mountain to make it move (Matthew 17:20). If you say "I have liver disease. I have only six months to live," then you *loose* satan to continue his attacks on your body.

On the other hand, you *bind* satan if you say, "Spirits of infirmity, you cannot stay in my body; you are defeated; I am healed according to God's Word." If you say, "I stand on God's Word" and "God declares Himself as the God who heals me" and "it is written to ask believing without doubt in my heart that I have already received it" and "nothing is impossible with God," then you allow God's healing power to make you whole.

Every single word you speak – *every single one* – is heard by God and also by satan. Who do you want working to fulfill your words? God asks you to choose Him and, therefore, to choose life.

Almighty God, I've been holding the keys of the kingdom in my hands and haven't understood how to use them. Now I know, and I bind the enemy in Jesus' name and guard my tongue so that I don't speak negatively to loose his destructive force. I speak Your words of healing and victory to allow Your mighty power to operate in my life. In Jesus' name, I pray, Amen.

✝

DAY 14
GOD'S WILL BE DONE ON EARTH

After this manner therefore pray ye: Our Father which art in heaven, Hallowed be thy name. Thy kingdom come. Thy will be done in earth, as it is in heaven. Give us this day our daily bread. And forgive us our debts, as we forgive our debtors. And lead us not into temptation, but deliver us from evil. For thine is the kingdom, and the power, and the glory, for ever. Amen. (Matthew 6:9-13)

Every Christian has repeated this prayer thousands of times. In fact, we often say it mechanically without even hearing the words or absorbing their meaning. What is this prayer about? Even though we call it "The Lord's Prayer," is it a prayer Jesus Himself would pray? No, because it includes a request for forgiveness for sins, and He was without sin. It was a prayer Jesus gave His disciples (who were not born again at the time) as an example of an appropriate way to pray.

Think of the number of times you have said, "Thy will be done in earth as it is in heaven." Stop for a moment to consider what God's will *is*, in fact, like in heaven. Do you believe there are intensive care units in heaven? Are people blind or deaf or hooked to kidney dialysis machines? Of course not. There is no sickness and disease in heaven. None. No deformities, no cancer, no mental illness, no heart disease, not even any warts. In heaven God's will is expressed perfectly.

God created the Garden of Eden to reflect the spiritual qualities of heaven and also to embody the physical realm. It was Adam and Eve's failure to stand against deception and their subsequent disobedience to God that led to sin, sickness, and disease.

In the Lord's Prayer, Jesus tells us to declare that God's will be manifested on earth just as it is manifested perfectly in heaven. Everything Jesus Himself did was in accordance with God's will. He healed every single person who came to Him and who wanted healing. He did that not just to convince people who He was, but He did it to fulfill His purpose of seeing that the Father's will was done in earth as it was in heaven.

Jesus told us that He followed the Father's will always, without ever deviating from it. Trust Jesus' words. Trust Jesus' actions. Pray the Lord's Prayer with feeling and with intent for your healing.

Heavenly Father, hallowed and blessed be Your name. May Your kingdom come. Your will be done in earth as it is in heaven. Give me this day my daily bread. And forgive me my debts, as I forgive my debtors. And let me not be led into temptation, but deliver me from the evil one. For Yours is the kingdom, and the power, and the glory for ever. In Jesus' name, I pray, Amen.

†

DAY 15
YOU CAN HAVE THE PETITIONS YOU ASK

And this is the confidence that we have in him, that, if we ask any thing according to his will, he heareth us: and if we know that he hear us, whatsoever we ask, we know that we have the petitions that we desired of him. (1 John 5:14-15)

Everywhere in the Scriptures we find one magnificent encouragement from God after another. But when I read this passage, I feel it is shouting time for sure!

"And this is the confidence that we have." Unshakeable confidence. We are to have no hesitation, no tentative "maybe," no cautious hoping. Instead, we begin with bold assurance and confidence. Confidence in whom? "In Him." In Jesus Christ, our Savior. The Apostle John, who wrote this Scripture, walked with our Lord, and he learned to have absolute confidence in Him by following Him faithfully.

Just as John knew that Jesus meant what He said, we must learn to trust that Jesus means what He says in the Word. We must trust Jesus to fulfill every promise and to do everything that He said He would do.

"If we ask any thing according to his will." Notice that what we are to ask has a qualification. Our requests are to be in line with the Word, which is the revealed will of God. This re-emphasizes the importance of resolving the underlying issue of knowing God's will for us. We have to know that we know that we know that it is God's will for us to be well. We have to know that we know that we know that our healing was won for us when Jesus defeated satan through the atonement of the Cross.

If we meet those conditions, then the Word says that God hears us. Wow! God, the Creator of the universe, our Heavenly Father, hears us. He hears you. He hears me. He hears every believer as we pray according to His will.

"And if we know that He hear us." A better translation of the Greek would be "*Since* we know that He hear us." We *know* that God hears us. We are sure. We are, in fact, guaranteed it right here in the Word. And what is it that God hears? Whatsoever we ask that is in accordance with His will.

Now look at the last part of verse 15: "We know that we have the petitions that we desired of Him." Does it say we should hope that we will get what we asked for? That's the way that most people actually pray. "Oh, God, if You want to, if it's Your will, I hope You will heal me, but if You don't heal me, I'll suffer bravely and see You in heaven." Does that kind of prayer line up with this Scripture in 1 John? No, it doesn't.

We are clearly told that we *have* the petitions we desire. That is something in the present rather than something in the future. You may say that you certainly don't see them. That may be the current circumstance in the physical realm, but remember that God is spirit. Everything begins first in the spiritual realm.

We must see with our spiritual eyes and believe in our heart that this Scripture is God's truth. And it says that, if we pray according to God's will, we have what we asked for. How could that be true? We first have the answers to our prayers in the spiritual realm and, as we line our thoughts and mind up to receive God's truth, then the results will manifest in our physical body.

This teaching is so radically different from current messages taught in the church that you may need to spend some time in prayer and meditation on these two verses. Ask the Holy Spirit to reveal the Father's truth to you so that you can begin to pray with the power of the Living Word.

Father God, I am excited by Your Word. I am excited that I can come boldly to Your throne with confidence. I know that Your Son has taken the stripes for my healing. For my healing. Father God, I know that it is Your will for me to be well. I have asked for specific organs in my body to be made whole. I declare that I now have what I have asked for. Help me to watch my words so that I speak only this truth from this day on. Thank You, Father. In Jesus' name, I pray, Amen.

†

DAY 16
THANK GOD IN ADVANCE

... And Jesus lifted up his eyes, and said, Father, I thank thee that thou hast heard me. And I knew that thou hearest me always: but because of the people which stand by I said it, that they may believe that thou hast sent me.

And when he thus had spoken, he cried with a loud voice, Lazarus, come forth. (John 11:41-43)

This is another powerful example for us in the way we are to pray for our healing. Lazarus, a dear friend of Jesus, has died, and Jesus arrives at his tomb after he has been buried for three days.

Notice what Jesus says when He prays. He doesn't beg God to bring Lazarus back to life. What He does is to thank God for hearing Him. Jesus says to God, "I know you always hear Me, but I'm saying this so the people standing here can hear Me, too." And because this is recorded in the Holy Scripture, Jesus was saying it for *your* benefit and for *your* ears. Notice that Jesus thanks God *in advance* for fulfilling His request. Lazarus' healing has not yet been manifested, but Jesus is saying "thank you" anyway.

That is what you must do. Are you waiting for your healing to manifest itself before you thank God for it? Gratitude must come before the manifestation. Why is this so important? Because thanks given in advance are based on your faith and your belief that God is indeed your healer and that the atonement of the Cross is a finished work.

If you are waiting for the manifestation to happen first, then you are, in fact, living in doubt that your healing is already done in the spirit realm. You may be *saying* "I believe" with your mouth, but you are *living* "I'll believe it when I see it" in your heart.

Jesus' faith was unshakable. Examine your own. What do you really believe? Lay your doubts at the feet of Jesus. Look to the Cross and then to the glory of the Resurrection, and say, "Thank you."

Father God, thank You for healing me. Thank You. I trust You, God, with all my heart. You are the Great Physician, my healer. Your Word says that when I pray according to Your will, You hear me. Thank You, God, for hearing me. Thank You, God, for being faithful to fulfill every promise and to keep Your covenant of healing with me. I believe, Father. I believe. And now that I have done all, I stand until my healing is fully manifested in my physical body. In the name of Your Son, Jesus Christ, my Redeemer and my Savior, I pray, Amen.

✝

DAY 17
THE POWER OF A PRAYER OF AGREEMENT

Again I say unto you, That if two of you shall agree on earth as touching any thing that they shall ask, it shall be done for them of my Father which is in heaven.   (Matthew 18:19)

There is enormous power in agreement. When we pray or speak in agreement with each other and when our words are in agreement with God's Word, then we know that the Most High God in heaven works to fulfill them. He sends His angels to have charge over us, and He moves to perform His Word because it can't return to Him void. God assures us that "My covenant will I not break" (Psalm 89:34).

But what happens if we agree in prayer about something that is contrary to what is written in the Word of God? Here's an example. Suppose a friend comes to visit and the two of us pray together, "God, if it is Your will, please heal me." What is God's response supposed to be? His Word clearly says that Jesus bore our sicknesses as a complete work two thousand years ago on the Cross.

I sometimes imagine that Father God might be thinking something like this. "My Word says that I want My will to be done on earth as it is in heaven, and no one is sick here with Me. My Word says that by the stripes of My Son she was healed. So why are My precious daughters questioning what I have already given?"

Remember that Jesus answered, "I will" when the leper asked for healing, "if thou wilt, thou canst make me clean" (Matthew 8:2). God cannot contradict Himself and He always keeps His Word. If He has already done something, already released a perpetual flow of grace and healing toward us, He can't act as though He hasn't done it. James teaches that it is the prayer of *faith* that saves, heals, and delivers the sick (James 5:15). A faith-filled prayer is one that is first and foremost in agreement with the Word of God.

Be aware of prayers you pray with others. Make sure that you join in agreement with faith-filled, Word-based petitions to the Almighty. The best prayers of all are to speak God's own words back to Him because He is always faithful to perform them.

Almighty God, I don't want to pray careless prayers anymore that don't line up with Your Word. From this day on I choose to join in agreement with others to pray according to Your revealed will that I be strong and healthy. I thank You, Father, for the completed work of the Cross, and I rejoice in knowing that by His stripes I was healed. In Jesus' name, I pray, Amen.

✝

DAY 18
SPEAK WHAT YOU WANT

... God, who quickeneth [gives life to] the dead, and calleth those things which be not as though they were. (Romans 4:17)

Paul tells us here in the Book of Romans that our God is the God who calls things that are not as though they were. In the beginning there was only chaos. This chaos was a fact, yet God saw beyond the appearance. God spoke, calling something that was not (a beautiful, orderly universe) as though it were. And from the power of His Word, He manifested a new creation that was His reality and His truth.

Paul gives us the example of Abraham to show us how we must get in agreement with God in "calling things that be not as though they were." Abram knew that he and Sarai were too old to have any children; those were the facts. Yet God made a promise to Abram and even changed his name to Abraham to seal it, saying, "Abraham, you will be the father of nations." God called something that was not (a mighty lineage descending from Abraham) as though it were. Then Abraham had to do the same thing in order for God's promise to manifest.

If you call things that are not as though they were, aren't you just wallowing in denial about your illness? The answer is no. Denial is pretending something does not exist. Look carefully at the words in Romans 4:17. You do not call something that *is* what is *not*. Instead, you call what is *not* as though it *were*.

Let me give you an example. Suppose the doctor's report is that your joint pain is due to arthritis. You don't say, "I was not diagnosed with arthritis" and put your faith in that statement. Why? Because the condition of arthritis exists at the physical level. You do not deny the diagnosis. What you deny is the right of that disease to stay in your body. Having heard the diagnosis, do not keep your attention focused there. Stop reinforcing the doctor's opinion by constantly voicing it.

Instead, ask yourself, "What is God's truth?" God is Jehovah-Rapha, the God who heals you. Jesus Christ bore every disease, including arthritis. God's will is that you be well and healthy. So speak in the way that God speaks. Call things that are not as though they were. Say, "I enforce God's Word on my joints and command them to be restored to normal, pain-free function. I declare my joints to be healthy according to God's design and purpose."

It does not matter if you look in the mirror and weary eyes look back at you. It does not matter if you feel discomfort in your body. Yes, these things exist in the physical realm. But you have a covenant promise from God and His words that are life and vitality. So, declare your faith in the God who gives life to the dead and calls things that are not as though they were. Look with your spiritual eyes and focus on God's reality which is beyond the appearance of your illness.

Do you see how this Scripture fits perfectly with 1 Peter 2:24, that by His stripes you were healed? Speak your wellness as though it were. Post this Scripture from Romans where you can read it and proclaim it out loud often. Let every cell in your body resonate with its truth. Receive the power of God and watch as your healing is manifested.

Father God, I hold onto Your Word which proclaims that You are the God who gives life to the dead and who calls things that are not as though they were. Nothing is impossible for You. I refuse to be sidetracked any more by symptoms I see and feel and touch because those things are not Your truth. I refuse to get sidetracked by bad reports from the doctor because Your Word says that the elders received a good report through their faith. I choose to look beyond the appearance of things to Your reality. My body is the temple for Your Holy Spirit, and I call every organ and cell whole and well in the name of Jesus. I call myself healthy from the top of my head to the bottom of my feet. Hallelujah! In Jesus' name, I pray, Amen.

†

DAY 19
SEEK GOD'S WAY FOR YOUR HEALING

Now Naaman ... was a leper. ... And Elisha sent a messenger unto him, saying, Go and wash in Jordan seven times, and thy flesh shall come again to thee, and thou shalt be clean. But Naaman was wroth, ... and said, Behold, I thought, He will surely come out to me, and stand, and call on the name of the Lord his God, and strike his hand over the place, and recover the leper.
(2 Kings 5:1, 10-11)

When people begin to see the revelation that healing has been provided in the atonement of the Lord Jesus Christ, they often question what form of healing is "right." Is it okay to go to the doctor for medical treatment? Is it all right to use herbs and essential oils? Is it evidence of a lack of faith in God to do anything in the physical realm? The answers are yes, yes, and no.

The first thing to remember is that God wants us well. He paid dearly for our healing through the stripes of His Son. What we need to avoid is acting like Naaman, who at first refused his healing because it didn't take the form that he thought it should take. He was angry because Elisha didn't even go out to see him. Then, when he was told to wash seven times in the river Jordan, he became even more furious because the Jordan was a very muddy, dirty-looking river. How could those waters possibly heal him?

Eventually he put his anger aside, became obedient, washed himself as he was instructed, and received his healing.

Too often we react just as Naaman did. We decide what our course of healing "should" look like. Usually, it follows the general pattern of going to a doctor, taking medication, having treatments, and perhaps undergoing surgery.

God always, always works with us where we are in our faith walk, and we are never condemned for choosing medical assistance in our healing. However, God requires that *He* be our Great Physician and primary consultant. He wants us to seek His guidance and allow the possibility that His plan may be something totally different from what we have considered previously. As in Naaman's case, it may even defy human logic and reason. Washing seven times in a dirty river in order to be healed seems ridiculous and stupid. Think of all the diseases you could *get* in a dirty river!

Don't sell God short. Don't hinder your healing by insisting that it be done *your* way. God has already released His healing power and it is yours to receive.

Almighty God, save me from being arrogant and stubborn. Give me an open mind so that I can be receptive to Your voice. I vow to consult You at every step along my path until my healing is manifested and to follow Your commands to me, no matter what they are or how unusual they seem. You are my Great Physician and Healer. In Jesus' name, I pray, Amen.

†

DAY 20
HERBS ARE GOD'S REMEDIES FOR HEALING

...and on either side of the river, was there the tree of life, which bare twelve manner of fruits, and yielded her fruit every month: and the leaves of the tree were for the healing of the nations. (Revelation 22:2)

In this description of the New Jerusalem, we see the tree of life, which was described in Genesis 2:9 as being in the Garden of Eden. From the beginning of all time (Genesis 1:29) to the end of all time, God has given a special place to the plant kingdom for the health of His children.

The more we learn about the function of the human body, the more we see how herbs, plants, and essential oils fit perfectly in the plan of human health. Science will never understand fully the value of herbs and plants to our health because it disregards all factors that can't be measured, tested, or seen. Herbs can be analyzed under a microscope, but they are much more than the sum of their chemical components. Why? Because they have in them the life of God. Since science ignores this very real truth, it sometimes draws conclusions that are either misleading or incomplete.

There are thousands and thousands of healing herbs and health-giving plants on our planet. These concentrated foods have been used since the beginning of time for our great benefit. It is tragic that most Americans today are

61

afraid to use God's remedies for healing because they mistakenly believe that what we humans have synthetically created is far better than what the Great Physician has created. Too many of us have forgotten that our scientific endeavors should flow from revelation knowledge and guidance from God and should complement rather than replace God's own remedies.

When using herbs and essential oils in your recovery process, seek instruction from the Holy Spirit, and be sure to give God all the glory for your healing rather than the herbs or essential oils. God has provided herbs, essential oils, and plants for us and for our healing in glorious, abundant profusion. Learn about them. Use them. But never forget that it is God and God alone who is your healer. Listen for God to speak to you. Then follow His guidance.

Wonderful Creator, thank You for the awesome abundance of herbs and plants which You have given me. Help me to learn about them and to use them in the way and for the purpose that You intended for my health and for my healing. Show me the herbs, plants, essential oils, and other natural remedies which You want me to use. I will do my part at the physical level, just as I receive Your healing power which You have released at the divine level. I give You all the glory for my healing. In Jesus' name, I pray, Amen.

†

DAY 21
IT IS WRITTEN

And when the tempter came to him, he said, If thou be the Son of God, command that these stones be made bread.

But he answered and said, It is written, Man shall not live by bread alone, but by every word that proceedeth out of the mouth of God.   (Matthew 4:3-4)

Jesus is our example. He shows us the way, tells us how to live, and demonstrates how to silence the voice of the enemy. Here in the fourth chapter of Matthew, the devil came to Jesus three times and repeatedly tried to tempt Jesus into violating the Word of God. Pay attention to the way that Jesus responded. He didn't argue or debate with satan or give him His own personal opinions. What He said was this: "It is written..." Three times His reply to satan was the Word of God.

The Word of God is to be our strength and our guide. "My covenant will I not break, nor alter the thing that is gone out of my lips" (Psalm 89:34). God says that His Word is an unshakeable rock, and He wants us to stand on it. This is especially important to remember when we feel weak, overwhelmed, and defeated. The enemy comes to us with whispers of temptation and most of all with whispers of doubt and fear. Satan knows that doubt and unbelief hinder the operation of our faith and weaken our trust in

God. Whenever he can get us to doubt God, he has interfered with our receiving the flow of the healing power of God in our lives.

Sickness is an excellent tool for satan to use to separate us from God. If he can get us to believe that God gave us sickness, he isolates us from God's will. If he can get us to doubt God's healing power, he keeps us focused on our symptoms and our illness.

Don't let satan succeed. Follow Jesus as He reminds us to live by "every word that proceedeth out of the mouth of God." That includes not only the written Word but also daily guidance. Listen for God's voice with an open heart and He will speak to you through the Holy Spirit. By staying focused on God's healing Word, it becomes easier and easier to speak your faith as healing is manifested in your body.

Heavenly Father, thank You for sending Your Son, Jesus, to teach me the way You want me to live. Thank You for reminding me to focus on Your Word. Whenever satan comes to separate me from You, help me to say, "It is written that I shall live by every Word that proceedeth out of the mouth of God." It is written that You are the God who heals me. I receive Your healing, and I thank You for restoring every cell, tissue, organ, and gland in my body to its proper function according to Your divine will. Thank You, Father. In Jesus' name, I pray, Amen.

†

Day 22
Fear Not

Be strong and of a good courage, fear not, nor be afraid of them: for the Lord thy God, he it is that doth go with thee; he will not fail thee, nor forsake thee.   (Deuteronomy 31:6)

Fear is your worst enemy. It is never from God; therefore, when you are filled with fear, you are in a place of separation from your Heavenly Father. Fear is satan's tool. Since it comes from the father of lies, you can be sure that it is always based on falsehood and deception.

Remember that satan is a defeated foe. No matter what the author of disease has done and no matter what sickness may befall us, God has already made provision for us. Through any disease and any adversity, we can say, "Fear not, for the Lord our God, it is He who goes with us."

We need not fear as we undergo medical treatment when we are being obedient to God's voice. Spirit-led doctors are wonderful and can be useful partners in our recovery process when God sends us to them. If we go for any other reason, we are operating from fear, and we are outside the plans that God has for us.

If we are sitting in the doctor's office, let it be because God told us to go and not because "everybody" thinks we should. If we are undergoing a particular surgery or treatment, let it be because God told us to do so and not because we were told by a doctor that we "have" to have it. Let God lead every step of the way and decide with finality all questions that arise in our healing process.

When God is your partner *and you are sure of it*, you are able to cast fear-attacks of the evil one far from you. When God is your partner *and you are standing on God's Word*, there is no room in your heart to be afraid.

When God is your partner *and you are filled with faith*, you know that you are safe. You know that you are a beloved child of God and that He will never fail you or forsake you. The peace that passes understanding will flood your soul, and you will rest in confidence and trust.

Almighty God, I stand in awe of the work of Your Son, Jesus Christ, who defeated the enemy and triumphed over him. Help me to be strong and of good courage. Your message is always, "Fear not, for I am with you." You are my shield and my salvation, my refuge and my strength. You go with me always, and You have promised never to fail or forsake me. In the name of Your Son, Jesus Christ, I pray, Amen.

✝

DAY 23
EMOTIONAL HEALING

For ye shall go out with joy, and be led forth with peace: the mountains and the hills shall break forth before you into singing, and all the trees of the field shall clap their hands.
(Isaiah 55:12)

What a delightful image it is for the hills to break forth singing and the trees to clap their hands! See that in your mind's eye. You can't help but smile.

Isaiah speaks to us of joy and of peace. When we feel ill, we often have little joy or peace, yet both are critical to our recovery. Healing isn't just about mending a broken bone or lowering a fever or normalizing blood pressure. It doesn't occur only at the physical level. Healing is a total experience of the complete person, and, therefore, it operates in the level of our soul (our mind, emotions, thoughts, and will) as well as our body.

One area that we often ignore is our emotional health. Many of us struggle throughout much of our lives with anger or grief or guilt or a myriad of other emotional issues. They burden our soul and damage our most valued relationships. But equally as harmful is the heavy toll that they take on our health by providing an environment at the physical level for disease to manifest.

Our language is filled with phrases that acknowledge our understanding of the relevance of our emotional health to our physical health. We speak of being "eaten up with guilt," "brokenhearted with grief," "scared to death," and "dying of loneliness."

In order to be well, we must be willing to let go of old hurts. Are you ready to be healed emotionally as well as physically? Are you ready to put away your resentment and anger once and for all? Are you ready to stop being a martyr and lay down your guilt once and for all? Are you ready to stop hiding in your grief once and for all?

God wants you to live singing with the hills and clapping your hands with the trees. And His Holy Word tells you that in addition to covering you with joy, your Heavenly Father wishes to lead you to His peace.

Dear Father, I have many old hurts that are painful to carry and yet are strangely comfortable. They have been a good hiding place, given me excuses for taking my pain out on others, and even allowed me to manipulate and control others. Forgive me, God, for carrying them so long. Help me to confront these emotional scars and to be set free. I want to be totally well and whole so that I live with joy and am led forth with peace. In Jesus' name, I pray, Amen.

✝

DAY 24
GOD'S BENEFITS

Bless the Lord, O my soul: and all that is within me, bless his holy name.

Bless the Lord, O my soul, and forget not all his benefits:

who forgiveth all thine iniquities; who healeth all thy diseases;

who redeemeth thy life from destruction; who crowneth thee with lovingkindness and tender mercies;

who satisfieth thy mouth with good things; so that thy youth is renewed like the eagle's.   *(Psalm 103:1-5)*

It is an eternal truth of God that forgiveness of sins and healing of the body are joined as God's gifts to us. Both are God's plan and God's will. His greatest desire is that we live in victory on earth and then join Him in eternity in heaven.

In this beautiful song of praise, David summarizes the great goodness of God. He lists six of the most extraordinary benefits provided by God that could ever be given. The first two are that God forgives all our iniquities and sins and heals all our diseases. Once again in Holy Scripture, we see the pairing of forgiveness of sins with healing.

Remember that David didn't live in the power of the shed blood of Jesus, so everything for him was in the present tense. He knew Jehovah as his Great Physician, the

God who heals. He could say as Isaiah did, "with his stripes we are healed" (Isaiah 53:5). For David, God forgives sins and God heals. David had to sacrifice continually and keep the law in order to feel righteous before God. Despite that, he acknowledged God as the healer of all disease. Not just some sicknesses, but all of them.

We are far more blessed than David. As marvelous as David's list is, we have the greatest benefit of all – the life, death, and resurrection of the Lord Jesus Christ. The Messiah was only a promise for David, but Jesus is a fulfilled reality for us. Through the atonement of the Cross, Jesus paid the price for our sins and for our sicknesses. Therefore, we joyfully proclaim, "by His stripes we *were* healed" (1 Peter 2:24).

Gather every ailment you are experiencing in an imaginary bundle in your hands and give them to your Lord Jesus Christ. See Him stretch out His arms and take them up. Hear Him say to you, "I have borne every one of these ailments and illnesses on the Cross for you. It is done. Now follow Me and be healed."

O Gracious God, You grant me so many blessings. Thank You for forgiving all my sins. Thank You for healing all my diseases. And thank You for redeeming my life from destruction. I accept these gifts with awe and gratitude. I receive my healing. Help me to be a faithful witness to others of Your magnificent glory. In Jesus' name, I pray, Amen.

✝

DAY 25
THE WORD OF GOD IS LIFE

It is the spirit that quickeneth; the flesh profiteth nothing: the words that I speak unto you, they are spirit, and they are life. (John 6:63)

These words were spoken by Jesus, and they can do exactly what Jesus says they can do – breathe life into us. Therefore, it is really important for us to take the time to study and meditate on the Word of God.

One essential tool is a concordance. My favorite is *Strong's Concordance*, which I use constantly. An online option is blueletterbible.org, which provides *Strong's Concordance* information at no cost to you.

When you find a verse in Scripture that speaks to you (or one that puzzles you), take the time to use your concordance to learn the full meaning of the words in the verse.

As an example, we learn that "quickeneth" means to vitalize or make alive. "Flesh" sometimes means just the body and other times it refers to human nature, which includes all of our emotions. Jesus tells us that it is the spirit that makes us alive, that vitalizes us. Contrary to that, the body and our human nature profit us nothing. Why would this be? Because God is spirit.

Jesus continues. "The words that I speak to you, they are spirit and they are life." Jesus was the Word itself. John 1:1 tells us that "in the beginning was the Word, and the Word was with God, and the Word was God."

His words are spirit because God is spirit. His words are life because God is the life-giver. They are life because Jesus died to defeat satan and to win perfect victory for us. If you turn the statement around, it says that you can't have life without His words.

That puts a large responsibility on each one of us to study His Word with passion and an open, seeking heart. Do you set aside time each day to read the Word and meditate on it? Meditating on the Word means both to study the Word (such as with a concordance or other reference materials) and to ask the Holy Spirit for revelation knowledge.

A Scripture that you have read a thousand times can suddenly leap off of the page and literally beat with the heart of God as you see a new truth for the first time. His words are *rhema*, which means that through the Living Word, the Lord speaks directly to you.

There is life-giving vitality in the Word. The Word of God is Spirit that calls out to your own born-again spirit. Seek out the declared will of God that is revealed in His Holy Word. Let it birth life in you.

Gracious Father, thank You for Your Holy Word which is spirit and life to me. I choose to spend more time seeking out Your truth and renewing my mind with Your Word. I want my words and my prayers to line up with Your Word, Father, and with Jesus' words which are life. In Jesus' mighty name, I pray, Amen.

✝

DAY 26
YOUR BODY IS THE TEMPLE
OF THE HOLY SPIRIT

What? know ye not that your body is the temple of the Holy Ghost which is in you, which ye have of God, and ye are not your own?

For ye are bought with a price: therefore glorify God in your body, and in your spirit, which are God's.   (1 Corinthians 6:19-20)

Here Paul reminds us that our bodies are holy. God designed our bodies and breathed into us the breath of life. How different our actions would be if we could keep focused on the fact that our bodies are temples. Every item we eat is really a prayer and an offering to God. Think about that the next time you open your mouth to eat.

The choice is ours whether to fill our temple with wholesome food that nourishes, builds, and fortifies our body or whether to trash it with unhealthy foods filled with toxins, antibiotics, hormones, and empty calories. We are offered more and more items that are called food but are either genetically altered, artificial, or chemically treated. We are sadly mistaken if we think that we can improve on God the Creator when it comes to our nourishment. We fill our bodies with junk, get sick, and then blame God by saying it was His will that we became ill.

Satan is the one who works to get us off the track by misleading us into making poor choices. He gets us to believe we can deceive our bodies with fake food and synthetic vitamins. How easy it is for him to get us to defile the temple.

Food isn't the only area of concern when we look at the issue of keeping our temple. We also honor our temple by giving it the proper exercise, by keeping it clean, and by following God's laws for appropriate sexual behavior within the sanctity of marriage.

Treat your body with the reverence due a creation of the Most High God. Treat it with the respect due the temple of the Holy Spirit. God has written your name on the palm of His hand, and you are His precious child. Because you were lost, He sent His Son to redeem you, spirit, soul, and body. You have been bought with a great price. Therefore, honor God with your body through every substance you eat and through every movement you make. When you do so, you join in partnership with God to create health, not only in your soul but also in your body.

Lord God, my life seems so hectic, and I let the "busy-ness" of life interfere with keeping my temple holy and healthy. Give me strength each day to follow Your instructions for healthy eating and healthy living. Help me to stay in partnership with You in honoring my body as the temple of the Holy Spirit. In Jesus' name, I pray, Amen.

✝

DAY 27
RESIST THE DEVIL

Submit yourselves therefore to God. Resist the devil, and he will flee from you. (James 4:7)

Too many Christians are sick and too many die because they don't understand this Scripture and act on it. First, we are told to "submit ourselves to God." In submitting to God's will for our life, we must have decided to believe the Word that it is God's will for us to be well. In numerous Scriptures God declares Himself as our healer, and He plainly tells us that He desires His will to be done on earth just as it is in heaven.

The next section of this passage in James tells us to "resist the devil." If we think that God gave us our illness, then we won't resist the devil because we haven't even identified him as part of the problem. Once we become aware that the enemy is the source of sickness, then we have to take the authority given to us in Luke 10:19 and use it against the devil. This a critical point that we often miss. Jesus said in Luke 10:19, "I give *you* power over all the power of the enemy." He said He gave it to *us*. That means He gave it to *you*. And to me. And to every believer.

The power is in His name and in the Word, but the responsibility is ours to use it. When we are hit with illness, we tend to act like victims and hand all responsibility for our healing over to God. "God, *You* do it," we say. "I'll just sit here and let You lay healing on me." But that's not what we see in the Word. God gives authority over the enemy to *you*. God tells *you* to resist the devil. He tells *you* to walk in the victory that has already been won for you. You are not the sick trying to get well. You are the healed who is under attack from the enemy.

Resist him. Confront your symptoms which are lies from the father of lies. With what? With the Word, the blood, and the name of Jesus. With the authority given to you in Luke 10:19 to command every symptom to leave. With the truth of 1 Peter 2:24 that by His stripes you were healed.

This is shouting time because the victory is yours. If you obey the commands of the Word, if you take your authority, and if you resist the devil, the enemy will flee. He must. Hallelujah!

Father God, I submit myself to You. I know without any doubt that it is Your will that I be whole and well. I resist the devil and in the name of Your Son, Jesus, I command every symptom of illness to leave my body. I command every organ and cell in my body to function perfectly in the name of Jesus and by the power of His shed blood. Thank You, Father. Thank You. In the precious name of Jesus, I pray, Amen.

†

DAY 28
YOUR EMOTIONS AFFECT YOUR PHYSICAL HEALTH

And there was delivered unto him the book of the prophet Esaias. And when he had opened the book, he found the place where it was written,

The Spirit of the Lord is upon me, because he hath anointed me to preach the gospel to the poor; he hath sent me to heal the brokenhearted, to preach deliverance to the captives, and recovering of sight to the blind, to set at liberty them that are bruised. ...

This day is this Scripture fulfilled in your ears.
(Luke 4:17-18, 21)

Physical illnesses are obvious to those who have them. What are not so obvious are emotional wounds. In order to be well, we have to understand the connection between our emotional and our physical health.

Jesus was very aware of the connection. He knew the effect of guilt and shame not only on a person's soul but also on his body. When someone who was sick came to Him, Jesus often said to him *first*, "Your sins are forgiven" and *then* told the lame to walk and the blind to see. Jesus came to set us at liberty. He came to heal the broken-hearted and to preach deliverance to the captives.

People who become ill often have an underlying anger, grief, shame, or fear. True healing cannot occur until these wounds are acknowledged and healed. Sometimes these hurts are buried very, very deeply because they are so painful. These wounds didn't come from God. They have accumulated through strife, loss, and hurtful life experiences. As a result, many of us have a myriad of negative emotions that the destroyer encourages us to hold onto. Don't keep struggling with your emotional scars. God has provided the solution and victory – deliverance through the authority of Luke 10:19.

Jesus came to heal the brokenhearted and to set at liberty those that are bruised. He wants you to be completely whole. He wants joy to reign in your heart. He smiles at you with compassion and offers His hand of deliverance, freedom, and peace.

Merciful Father, I have become trapped by many memories and old hurts from the past. They are heavy and painful to carry, and I have allowed them to steal my peace and my joy. Forgive me for holding onto anger, bitterness, grief, regret, jealousy, pride, rejection, and a hundred other negative emotions. I am ready to let them go. Thank You for sending Your Son to heal my broken heart and to bring me deliverance so that I can walk in freedom and joy according to Your purpose and will. In the name of Jesus Christ, my Savior, healer, and deliverer, I pray, Amen.

†

Day 29
Your Body Hears What You Say

Let the words of my mouth, and the meditation of my heart, be acceptable in thy sight, O Lord, my strength, and my redeemer. (Psalm 19:14)

Do the words that come out of your mouth describe the life you want to live? Imagine that some kind of recorder was running and retaining every single comment, word, and thought. Does that thought make you cringe a little? Well, the fact is that there is such a recording, a heavenly recording. And some day there will be an accounting, even for every idle word.

There is another recording happening which is producing an immediate earthly accounting. This is occurring in your body. Each cell hears everything you say and will accept what you say and think as the truth. It will conform to your words just as you speak them or think them.

We shape our world with our words. The Holy Scripture tells us repeatedly how vital and how powerful the Word of God is. Our own words have great power as well. If we constantly speak negative thoughts, we open the door to the enemy because we are giving negative instructions to our own organs.

Listen to yourself today. Do you find yourself saying things such as, "I'll never get well"? Or "This pain in my back is killing me." Do these words describe the life that you really want for yourself? If not, as soon as they slip out of your mouth, say, "Cancel that." Say it out loud if at all appropriate. If not, just think it.

Then rephrase the sentence and say the revised words out loud. For example, "I call my liver whole and healthy in the name of Jesus." Or "It is written that I was healed by the stripes of Jesus." Or "Pain, by the authority of Luke 10:19 I command you to leave my body now. Spine, you straighten up and operate easily and comfortably."

When are the words of our mouth acceptable offerings to God? When they line up with His will and His purpose for us. When they are words of truth. When they are filled with praise and thanksgiving for His blessings. When they agree with Holy Scripture. Monitor your words and thoughts one day at a time and then make the changes you need. Align your words with God's Word and God's truth so that they create an atmosphere of love and faith around you.

Let the words of my mouth and the meditation of my heart be acceptable in Your sight, O Lord God, my strength, and my redeemer. When my words line up with Your will and Your purpose for my life, then I know they are acceptable to You. Help me to be aware of my words and of their power. In the name of Your Son, Jesus Christ, I pray, Amen.

✝

Day 30
Will You Be Made Whole?

When Jesus saw him lie, and knew that he had been now a long time in that case, he saith unto him, Wilt thou be made whole? (John 5:6)

"Do you want to be made whole?" Doesn't this seem to be a strange question? Who would answer, "No"? Yet if you read further in this text, you will see that the man didn't reply "yes" to Jesus' question. Instead, he began telling Jesus all the reasons why he hadn't been able to get into the healing waters.

People are no different today from the way they were then. Many of us may say we want to be well, and yet we are actually afraid of living. We put on a brave front and create an outward appearance of "normalcy," even though inside we feel afraid, lonely, and wounded.

The truth is that sickness offers a hiding place that seems safe to us. It may provide a reason to withdraw from others. Or it may give us a reason to ask for support and for loving care that we aren't able to ask for when we are healthy. Or it may provide a physical focus so that we don't have to deal with our emotional and spiritual issues. Oddly enough, in these and in many other ways, feeling sick actually serves some purpose for us.

Jesus came to heal us totally. He came to heal our souls and He came to heal our bodies. When He looked at the man lying at the pool at Bethsaida, Jesus knew He could heal him. But He also knew that the man must not only want to be well but also be willing to change his old thoughts and behaviors.

As Christians, we are used to saying to Jesus, "I believe that my spirit is saved and that I am going to heaven, so I don't fear death." Now we must learn to say, "I also believe You have redeemed my body from illness through the stripes You took, and, therefore, I do not fear *life* in full service to You."

Look into your heart now. Search out all the possible reasons why being ill serves some purpose for you, list them on paper, and then decide if you are ready to live without them. If so, offer them to God. Destroy the list and tell satan, "It is written that Christ Jesus took all my infirmities and bore all my sicknesses. The victory has been won for me. Every symptom of sickness must leave my body now. I receive my healing. Hallelujah!"

Yes, Father God, I want to be well. Yes. Remove from me all blocks to my mental, emotional, and physical healing. Deliver me from all old hurts, wounds, and behaviors which separate me from You. Take my fears and my doubts. I receive Your blessings, Father, as I choose to live, to be well, and to serve You. In Jesus' name, I pray, Amen.

†

Day 31
Disciples Are to Heal, Deliver, and Preach

After these things the Lord appointed other seventy also, and sent them two and two before his face into every city and place, whither he himself would come. Therefore said he unto them,

... heal the sick that are therein, and say unto them, The kingdom of God is come nigh unto you. (Luke 10:1-2, 9)

Here we see Jesus as He trains those who are to carry on His work. The picture is an interesting one because Jesus' church isn't a church of buildings or a cumbersome bureaucracy. It is simply people going out two by two under the direction of the Lord. They were given specific things to do: to heal, deliver, and preach the Gospel. Over and over in the Gospels we see these same commands given. Heal, deliver, and preach. Heal, deliver, and preach. This is what I call true discipleship at work.

Seventy people. What kind of people? Scripture doesn't indicate that there was anything particularly remarkable about this group of followers whom Jesus sent to act in His behalf. There is no mention of their being well-educated or having medical training. They were apparently "ordinary" believers who were sent to preach and to heal.

This is the way the church is to act and to look now. Mark 16:20 says, "And they went forth, and preached every where, the Lord working with them, and confirming the word with signs following." This should still be happening today. Where believers are gathered in the name of Jesus, there should be signs and wonders of people recovering their health since Jesus put healing on the same level as preaching. Where there was one, there was always the other.

The two actions work in tandem with each other. Healing and preaching make a complete unit because it takes both of them to meet people's complete needs. Jesus came to make us whole. He came to do the perfect will of the Father and to redeem us to God's original intent for us.

Jesus sits today at the right hand of the Father and *still* desires for us to walk in the wholeness that He died to obtain for us. He went to the Cross to atone for our sins *and* our sicknesses. What is required is that we believe that this is so and act on it.

Gracious God, thank You for showing me the way. Help me to understand in the deepest parts of my soul and in the innermost places of my heart that You sent Your precious Son to atone for me completely, for my spirit, soul and body. Father God, Your Word tells me that Jesus sent out believers, just ordinary people like me, to preach the Gospel and to heal the sick. I don't want to waste another day. Help me to be an instrument for the healing of others right now. Help me to join with those whom Jesus sent out then and sends out now to do His work. In Jesus' name, I pray, Amen.

†

DAY 32
YOU ARE SURROUNDED
BY HEAVENLY HELP

And he answered, Fear not: for they that be with us are more than they that be with them.

And Elisha prayed, and said, Lord, I pray thee, open his eyes, that he may see. And the Lord opened the eyes of the young man; and he saw: and, behold, the mountain was full of horses and chariots of fire round about Elisha.   (2 Kings 6:16-17)

What a great movie this story would make. The king of Syria is at war with Israel, but every time he begins an attack, he finds the king of Israel already has his forces in place. After this happens repeatedly, he summons his staff together and demands to know who the spy is.

One of his servants tells him that there is no Syrian traitor but that Elisha, the prophet of Israel, knows the words the king speaks in his own bedchamber and that the prophet is telling this information to the king of Israel. Naturally, the king of Syria sends forces out to capture Elisha. Elisha's servant wakes up one morning, goes outside, and sees that he and Elisha are surrounded by a "great host" of Syrian horses, chariots, and warriors. He is terror-stricken and rushes to Elisha in a panic.

Elisha has an advantage over his servant. He has the capacity to look at circumstances with spiritual eyes instead of just with physical eyes. He was certain of God's protection even though it looked as though they were completely outnumbered by the enemy. "Relax," Elisha told his servant. "There are more of us than there are of them."

Can you imagine the expression on the servant's face? He is thinking, "There is Elisha and there is me. That makes two of us. And I can see more chariots than I can count. Is this guy crazy?"

Elisha then asks God to open his servant's spiritual eyes. To the man's astonishment, he sees that "the mountain was full of horses and chariots of fire round about Elisha." Victory was already assured, but the servant didn't believe it until he saw it.

Don't be deceived by appearances. The enemy is the father of lies. You should never ignore symptoms, but you must see the victory of the blood of the Cross with your spiritual eyes. Your chariots of fire are activated when you enforce the Word of God on your body and take authority over the enemy who is attacking you. Fear not, for they that be with *you* are far more than they that be against you.

Almighty God, help me to keep my spiritual eyes open to the truth of Your victory. Help me see myself as completely healthy according to Your Word. I will share my testimony with others so that they, too, can walk in the power and authority that You have given to us. In Jesus' name, I pray, Amen.

†

DAY 33
IT IS FINISHED

When Jesus therefore had received the vinegar, he said, It is finished: and he bowed his head, and gave up the ghost. (John 19:30)

"It is finished," Jesus said in His last statement on the Cross. It is finished. The translation in *The Message* says, "It's done ... complete."

The Greek word used for "it is finished" is *tetelestai*. There is an interesting use of this word which enriches our understanding of this Scripture. During Jesus' time on earth, prison records contained an official document showing the number of years of the sentence that each person had to serve in jail.

Suppose a man committed a crime and was sentenced for three years. At the end of the first year, a notation would be made that year one had been completed, and likewise, a similar notation would be made at the end of year two. Finally, at the end of the third and final year, the paper would be stamped or marked, "tetelestai." Paid in full. And the man would be set free.

Paid in full. Completed. Finished. That's what Jesus did for us. He paid everything in full for us. He took our place and it pleased God to bruise Him instead of us. By atoning for every one of our sins, He set us totally free.

Paul uses a similar analogy in Colossians 2:14 when he writes that Jesus "blotted out the handwriting of ordinances that was against us, which was contrary to us, and took it out of the way, nailing it to his cross." He accomplished once and for all our "*soteria*" (the noun that comes from the Greek word "*sozo*") – our salvation, our healing, our deliverance, our being made whole.

This is the reason that 1 Peter 2:24 uses the past tense to say that "by His stripes we *were* healed." It is finished. It is complete. The atonement of the Cross pays off in full every ordinance that is contrary to us.

The defeat of the enemy is total. Our enemy is neither dead nor sleeping, but he *is* defeated. We must follow Jesus' command not to be hearers only but also doers of the Word. When we take action, we walk in the victory of the blood of Jesus.

Father God, words cannot adequately express my gratitude for the victory won for me by Jesus on the Cross. He paid every price for me in full. He took the stripes on His back so that I can walk in healing. He claimed the keys of death and hell so that I will live eternally in heaven. Father, forgive me when I grow weary of resisting the enemy. Help me to be bold, to take my authority that Jesus purchased through His blood, and to enforce the Word on every cell in my body. I praise Your name and glorify You. In the mighty name of Jesus who shed His precious blood for me, I pray, Amen.

✝

DAY 34
GOD DOES NOT LIE

... yea, let God be true, but every man a liar. (Romans 3:4)

God is not a man, that he should lie; neither the son of man, that he should repent: hath he said, and shall he not do it? or hath he spoken, and shall he not make it good? (Numbers 23:19)

He that believeth on the Son of God hath the witness in himself: he that believeth not God hath made him a liar; because he believeth not the record that God gave of his Son. (1 John 5:10)

When life is going well, it is easy to say that we trust God. When everything seems to be going smoothly, it's easy to say that we believe His Word. But what happens when the circumstances around us don't seem to be lining up with what the Word says?

Suppose you've been coughing for several weeks and you go to the doctor for a check-up. It's probably some stubborn little bug, he says, but he runs a few tests. You get a phone call asking you to come to the office. Immediately you feel fear because you know the report isn't going to be good. With a grim face, he tells you, "It's cancer." He shows you the report. It has been checked and double-checked. The diagnosis is clear.

Who told you that cancer is in your body? The doctor. Is the doctor a human or God? Clearly a human. The doctor has given you the best that he has; however, he is

91

limited to the physical realm in presenting his report. But God is a spirit being and has already released His healing power in the spiritual realm. He says through the writer of Hebrews 11:2, by faith "the elders obtained a good report."

Now is the time for you to exercise your faith and obtain your own good report. Look with spiritual eyes at spiritual truth. God is always the God of truth. He can't lie in His Word. He simply can't lie.

If God's Word says that by His stripes you *were* healed, then that means that God does not see you as a sick person. Through the blood of Jesus He sees you as a well person being attacked. It is critical that you see yourself exactly the same way that God sees you, so see yourself well with your spiritual eyes.

God wants you to take the authority of Luke 10:19 and command that illness to leave. He wants you to receive your healing now.

Father God, I have received a bad report about my health from man. You are God and You can't lie. You have spoken through Your Word and You fulfill everything in it. You have spoken and You make Your Words good. You are the God of truth and it is written that by the stripes of Jesus I am healed. I receive my healing now. In the name of Jesus, I pray, Amen.

†

Day 35
Prosper and Be in Health

Beloved, I wish above all things that thou mayest prosper and be in health, even as thy soul prospereth. For I rejoiced greatly, when the brethren came and testified of the truth that is in thee, even as thou walkest in the truth. I have no greater joy than to hear that my children walk in truth. (3 John 1:2-4)

In this letter of the Apostle John to Gaius, the leader of one of the early Christian churches, John offers encouragement and support. Around A.D. 85 opposition to the Christians was increasing and certain people who had joined the church were causing trouble. John is eager to remind his friends of Christ's teachings and of their mission to spread the Gospel.

John begins his letter with a prayer that Gaius be in good health. I want you to prosper and be healthy just as your soul prospers. That is the Word from the Lord through the apostle. Some people believe this is a social pleasantry, similar to our saying, "Hope you're doing fine."

However, John is equating the health of Gaius' soul with his physical health and his prosperity. This is the same concept embraced in the Greek word, "*sozo*", which means to do well, to save, to heal, to deliver, and to make whole. It's a complete package.

Gaius is a church leader, and John knows that physical vitality is important in doing the work of the Lord. Certainly people can be wonderful witnesses no matter what the state of their health, but obviously a healthy person has more energy and mobility than someone who is ill. And a healthy person is a living witness of 1 Peter 2:24 and Matthew 8:17.

If being sick were to be a model for our service to God, then surely Jesus would have left unhealed some of those who came to Him. Or Jesus Himself might even have suffered some ailment. He shared every other obstacle and difficulty that we face as human beings. Isn't it interesting that illness was the only one that He didn't share with us until He took our sicknesses on Himself through the stripes on His back?

Live your own life as an example of what it is to walk minute by minute in God's truth, having the courage to follow God's guidance and to depend on Him totally and completely.

Father God, I stand on Your Word which declares that I prosper and be in health just as my soul prospers. You said that the harvest is plenteous but the laborers are few. I want to be a vigorous laborer for You, and I want my life to be a shining witness for Your Word. I want to walk in Your truth and in the victory won on the Cross for me by Your Son, Jesus Christ, in whose name I pray, Amen.

†

DAY 36
BELIEVE YOU HAVE WHAT YOU SAY

... Have faith in God. For verily I say unto you, That whosoever shall say unto this mountain, Be thou removed, and be thou cast into the sea; and shall not doubt in his heart, but shall believe that those things which he saith shall come to pass; he shall have whatsoever he saith. Therefore I say unto you, What things soever ye desire, when ye pray, believe that ye receive them, and ye shall have them. (Mark 11:22-24)

When you feel sick or have been injured, your health problem seems like a mountain. A BIG mountain. Jesus told us not to worry about mountains in our path because, if we have faith, we can accomplish anything. It is interesting that in this Scripture, Jesus tells us to talk to the mountain, saying, "Be thou cast into the sea."

Once again in Scripture we are shown how important *words* are - not only God's Holy Word but also our own. Through them we voice either our authority over the situations in our life or our fears and helplessness to them. Jesus teaches us to clarify our intent and announce it firmly and succinctly because we "shall have whatsoever we saith."

Equally important is to remove doubt and unbelief from your heart. Why is this so important? Doubt is the handiwork of satan and separates us from our Heavenly Father. When we entertain doubt in our thoughts or when we voice it in our conversations, we are allowing satan to undermine our faith.

A key point here in Jesus' teaching is to believe that you have already received what you have spoken in your prayer. This is a reinforcement of the Holy Scripture that declares that God "calls those things which are not as though they were" (Romans 4:17). God Himself speaks what He knows is true in the spiritual realm as though it is already present in the physical realm. Here Jesus is telling us to pray the same way.

Pray, believing you receive what you desire, Jesus tells us. You must believe *before* you see the manifestation of what you want. You must believe even though the appearance says that nothing seems to have changed. You must believe even if the appearance seems to be getting worse.

With that kind of faith, you can tell a mountain to be cast into the sea and it must obey. Tell your mountain of diabetes to be removed. Tell your mountain of cancer to leave you. Tell your mountain of heart disease to go in Jesus' name. Call every organ in your body healthy in the name of Jesus. Now believe that you have received those things that you have spoken.

Father God, forgive me for the times when I have faltered and let fear overtake me. Strengthen me so that I don't doubt in my heart, but instead I pray, believing that I receive the healing I desire. I speak to my mountain now and command it to go. I stand on Your Word, knowing that by Jesus' stripes I was healed. In the glorious name of Jesus, I pray, Amen.

✝

DAY 37
HOW TO PRAY

For this cause I bow my knees unto the Father of our Lord Jesus Christ, of whom the whole family in heaven and earth is named,

That he would grant you, according to the riches of his glory, to be strengthened with might by his Spirit in the inner man;

That Christ may dwell in your hearts by faith; that ye, being rooted and grounded in love,

May be able to comprehend with all saints what is the breadth, and length, and depth, and height;

And to know the love of Christ, which passeth knowledge, that ye might be filled with all the fullness of God. (Ephesians 3:14-19)

Compare this prayer of Paul with your own and with prayers you hear others pray. There is no begging God to fix people in this prayer, no whining about how bad the world situation is, no endless pleading to please bring revival. Even though it is addressed to the Ephesians, it is also written as a prayer specifically for us.

What did Paul pray? First, he prayed that we would be strengthened with might by the Holy Spirit in our inner man. Why? Because it is power that gives us boldness to take authority over the enemy. It is might and courage that enables us to carry the love of Christ to a hurting world.

Second, he prayed that we would know the love of Christ for us. Why? Because only through that knowledge can we begin to understand how much He has provided for us through His sacrifice on the Cross.

Third, he prayed that we would be filled with all the fullness of God. He did not ask God to give us something more or to do something more. He prayed that we would receive the fullness that God already is and that God has already done. Do you see the difference?

We too often ask God to move. God, do something. God, the world is a mess. God, fix it. God, bring revival. We act as though God has done very little for us because we are always asking for Him to do something else.

We are revival. Revival should go wherever we go. We are the church. The good news of the Lord should go wherever we do. We are the healed. Signs and wonders should follow us, just as they accompanied the believers of the early church. We are saved, healed, delivered, prospered, and made whole. It is time that we received what has already been given.

Father God, forgive me for not understanding what You have done for me through the atonement of the Cross. I ask to be strengthened with might by the Holy Spirit in my inner man. I ask that I may comprehend the love of Christ for me. And I ask that I be filled with all the fullness of God. Thank You, Father. In Jesus' name, I pray, Amen.

†

DAY 38
THE POWER THAT WORKS IN YOU

Now unto him that is able to do exceeding abundantly above all that we ask or think, according to the power that worketh in us,

Unto him be glory in the church by Christ Jesus throughout all ages, world without end. Amen.   (Ephesians 3:20-21)

This passage of Scripture completes the prayer of Paul that we just discussed. Let me write it the way most of us have learned it. "Now unto him that is able to do exceeding abundantly above all that we ask or think." We stop right there, leaving off the clause that says, "according to the power that worketh in us."

That little change makes a world of difference. Is God able to do exceeding abundantly above all that we ask or think? Absolutely. He is our loving Father and He wants the very best for us.

But to stop there shifts all the responsibility for action to God. It allows us to stay in a "whatever will be, will be" passive position of patient waiting. Did you realize that "waiting on the Lord" has more of the meaning of giving constant attention as a restaurant waiter serves and "waits on" his customer than it does of sitting down and passively letting time go by?

Let's press on and look at verse 20 in its entirety. The words "according to" provide a qualification to God's ability to do exceeding abundantly above all that we ask or think. Paul says that God's action is according to the power that works in us. According to the power that He has given to us? No. According to the power that waits in us? No. According to the power that *works* in us.

The Greek word for power in this verse is *dunamis*, from which we get the word "dynamite." It means force, violence, strength, and miraculous power. God has given us miracle-working power which is totally useless until we activate it and make it work in us and through us. When we take action with the *dunamis* of God inside us, then and only then is God able to do exceeding abundantly above all that we ask or think. When we are willing to take our delegated authority, then God has a useful servant in whom He can show Himself strong.

Step up to the plate. You have the sword of the Spirit in your hands. Use your *dunamis* and watch the miracles flow!

Father God, thank You for giving me dunamis power. I want it to work in me for Your glory and Your honor. I want to use it to demonstrate Your great love for Your children. Help me to be bold, Father, to light the fuse of the power You have entrusted to me. In the name of my Lord Jesus Christ, I pray, Amen.

✝

Day 39
God Gives Good Gifts

Or what man is there of you, whom if his son ask bread, will he give him a stone? Or if he ask a fish, will he give him a serpent?

If ye then, being evil, know how to give good gifts unto your children, how much more shall your Father which is in heaven give good things to them that ask him? (Matthew 7:9-11)

What mother would choose to give her child leukemia to teach him to be more obedient? What father would cripple his son in order to teach him patience? Only a very few mentally ill parents would do such horrendous things. Yet we often accuse God of these hurtful acts. "It's His will," we say. "God is sovereign," we say.

Is God sovereign and all-powerful? Of course. But read Genesis 1:26. God sovereignly limited His sovereignty by giving dominion "over all the earth" to man. When He created His beloved children, He didn't want puppets, forced to do His bidding. He wants us to *choose* to love Him and to race into His embrace because we *want* to, not because we *have* to.

God isn't an erratic, unknowable God. He wants us to know Him intimately, so much so that He has placed Himself in the person of the Holy Spirit within us. Furthermore, He has set forth in His Holy Word exactly what control He has delegated to us. And He says that He will not break His covenant.

By saying that God is totally sovereign and ignoring the dominion He delegated to us, we shift the responsibility for every event to Him. Taking responsibility is work, so it is much easier to hand that job over to God. We would rather believe that God controls every single event that happens to us.

But every action of every person is not willed by God. He hates sin and could never direct people to do what He abhors. If God is responsible for all sicknesses and trage-dies because they serve some purpose, then satan must be as bored and as idle as the Maytag man.

God is a good God. He is the source of every blessing. He loves you dearly and has provided that you be well and strong in service to Him.

Father God, I won't blame You anymore for the devil's work and my own failures. You haven't handed me a serpent, which is the symbol of the devil, but You have given me a fish, which is the symbol of Jesus Christ. You have chosen to give me huge authority by delegating dominion over all the earth and all the power of the enemy. Help me to use this power appropriately, consistently, and wisely. Help me to walk in the victory that was won by Your Son through His shed blood. In the mighty name of Jesus, I pray, Amen.

✝

DAY 40
USE THE FAITH YOU HAVE

And the apostles said unto the Lord, Increase our faith.

And the Lord said, If ye had faith as a grain of mustard seed, ye might say unto this sycamine tree, Be thou plucked up by the root, and be thou planted in the sea; and it should obey you.
(Luke 17:5-6)

How do you rate your faith level? Low, medium, or high? Do you think you have enough faith to receive your healing? If you aren't experiencing the results that you want, you may do as many of us do and compare yourself to various people in the Bible. You end up excusing yourself because you believe you just don't have as much faith as they did.

I suppose the disciples must have been constantly tempted to compare themselves to Jesus and to despair of matching the faith that they witnessed in Him. In this passage in Luke, the disciples make a direct request of Jesus to increase their faith.

Look at Jesus' reply. He tells them that they need only a tiny-sized faith to do what "normal" people would consider to be totally impossible. Even in today's world of instant computer messaging, the idea of commanding a tree to jump up out of the ground, roots and all, leap over to the sea, and then implant its roots underwater sounds like science fiction.

Jesus essentially told the disciples to use the faith that they already had. He gave no instruction on how to get more faith. He didn't give a sermon called "5 Ways to Increase Your Faith." Instead, He said, use what you've got and you can do miracles.

He illustrated His point by telling the story of a master and a servant, which is easier for us to understand in our culture in terms of an employer-employee relationship. What employer would do the work of his employee because he felt sorry for him or thought he had already worked long enough? None would. The employee (or servant) is expected to work to benefit the employer.

Our faith is like the employee and is supposed to work to benefit us by fulfilling everything the Word says and everything that Jesus died to give us. We do not need to rate our faith level or to beg for more faith. We simply need to use what we have.

Father God, I know that I have often called on You to increase my faith. I make a decision now to use the faith that I have. I choose to exercise my spiritual "muscle" of faith just as Jesus told me to do. I look with my spiritual eyes at Your truth, and I triumphantly proclaim my divine health. I glorify and thank You, Father, that I am blessed. In the precious name of Jesus, I pray, Amen.

☦

Day 41
The Measure of Faith

... according as God hath dealt to every man the measure of faith.
(Romans 12:3)

Another reason we don't have to strive to "get" faith is this assurance in the Word that, when we were born again, God Himself gave us our measure of faith. God is our complete provider and He has never, ever left us short-changed in anything that we need. Faith is essential, so He Himself has deposited it within us at the time of our salvation, just as He deposited the Holy Spirit within us.

Some scholars say that the Scripture says "a" measure of faith rather than "the" measure of faith. Rather than getting caught up in a dispute over different translations, let's concentrate on the fact that God has given faith to each one of us. He is not a "respecter of persons" (Acts 10:34), which means that He doesn't discriminate among those who believe in Him. Therefore, just as it is not true that some of us are given more of the Holy Spirit than others, it also is not true that some of us are given more faith than others.

What is different is what we do with what we are given. Some people develop their relationship with the Holy Spirit and learn how to hear His voice. Others hardly recognize Him and they flounder endlessly in struggle after struggle. They could have walked in the victory that comes through the guidance of the Holy Spirit, but they did not get to know Him.

The same thing is true with faith. God has given faith to us. We didn't earn it. We didn't work for it. It was a gift when we were born again (Ephesians 2:8). Once we have it, we are to use it. We have to exercise our faith muscles just as we build up our physical muscles.

Scripture lists the "roll-call" of faith in Hebrews 11. One person after another is listed who simply took God at His Word. If God said it, then they believed it, no matter how outrageous it seemed. A ninety-year-old woman believed she would have a baby. A man who had never seen rain in his life believed that water would fall from the sky and flood the earth. Another man allowed himself to be led into what looked like certain death, trapped between an Egyptian army and water too wide to get the entire people of Israel across.

All of these people used the faith they had and believed God. Follow their example, exercise your measure of faith, and watch miracles happen.

Father God, thank You for my measure of faith. It is Your gift to me, and from today onward, I will exercise it and grow it by standing on Your Word in belief and trust. Thank You, Father. In Jesus' name, I pray, Amen.

✝

Day 42
The Light of God's Word

Thy word is a lamp unto my feet, and a light unto my path.
(Psalm 119:105)

How do we keep His light shining brightly in our lives? By following His Holy Word, which is truly the lamp unto our feet and the light unto our paths. God's Word is available in Holy Scripture, and it is also revealed when He speaks to us directly.

When you are ill or injured, you need the illumination of God's Word to keep you grounded in God's truth for you. It is easy to be swept up in the appearance of your condition and to be swayed by the well-meaning advice of others.

This is the time to turn to God's Word. Read it, breathe it, swim in it! Seek out the revelation of God's will in the life, words, and ministry of His Son, Jesus Christ. Notice that Jesus referred often to God's Holy Word and that His rebuke to satan was "It is written, it is written, it is written."

Repeat the Word to yourself many times each day. It is written, "I am the Lord that healeth thee" (Exodus 15:26). It is written, "Thy faith hath made thee whole" (Mark 10:52). It is written, "Himself took our infirmities, and bare our sicknesses" (Matthew 8:17).

It is written, "If ye have faith as a grain of mustard seed, ye shall say unto this mountain, Remove hence to yonder place; and it shall remove; and nothing shall be impossible unto you" (Matthew 17:20). It is written, "And great multitudes followed him, and he healed them all" (Matthew 12:15). It is written, "Bless the Lord, O my soul, and forget not all his benefits: who forgiveth all thine iniquities; who healeth all thine diseases" (Psalm 103:2-3).

Sometimes there are passages that you may not understand. Don't spin in your confusion because satan is particularly eager for you to discard Holy Scripture as your guidepost. Seek guidance from believers who are walking in the fullness of everything that was provided in the atonement, study on your own, and then turn your frustration over to God. Ask for revelation knowledge to clear your mind and your heart, to light your way, and to bring you to God's truth.

Almighty and merciful Father, thank You for Your wonderful Holy Word. It is indeed a lamp unto my feet and a light unto my path. It is You, speaking to me; therefore, it is my best and truest source of inspiration. It gives me examples of real people in real situations who kept the faith and remained steadfastly obedient to You. It shows me how You poured Your love over Your children in countless acts of mercy and grace. Thank You for this great gift of Your Word which I cherish in my heart. In Jesus' name, I pray, Amen.

✝

DAY 43
THE POWER OF GIVING THANKS

Then Jonah prayed unto the Lord his God out of the fish's belly, and said, I cried by reason of mine affliction unto the Lord, and he heard me; out of the belly of hell cried I, and thou heardest my voice. ...

The waters compassed me about, even to the soul: the depth closed me round about, the weeds were wrapped about my head. ... Yet hast thou brought up my life from corruption, O Lord my God. ...

But I will sacrifice unto thee with the voice of thanksgiving; I will pay that that I have vowed. Salvation is of the Lord.
(Jonah 2:1-2, 5-6, 9)

If you are experiencing serious illness, you understand Jonah. This is particularly true if you have been diagnosed with a disease which modern medicine pronounces incurable because it is easy for despair to set in. Treatment options offered are often a double-edged sword. While appearing to slow one health problem, they often lead in the end to creating another. So there you are, feeling as if you are deep in the belly of the giant fish, just like Jonah.

What did Jonah do? He calls to God, saying, "You heard me and You answered me, God." *Past* tense. Remember that *he is still in the belly of the fish!* The appearance is that he is still trapped and that his situation is hopeless. Yet Jonah then sings a song of thanksgiving! Even though it looks as though he is still doomed, here he is loudly thanking God for saving him. He trusts God completely, so much so that he sees his deliverance as *already* accomplished. It is only *after* he does these things that he is saved from the fish.

You can do something that Jonah couldn't do. You can look to the Cross and speak the words, "by His stripes I was healed" (1 Peter 2:24). But be like Jonah in knowing that God hears you and has already provided for your healing.

Find music of thanksgiving and praise and sing along with it every day. A great free resource online is soulkeeperradio.com where you can get Christian music 24/7 every day of the year. With music, song, and exultation, rejoice and look with your spiritual eyes at the salvation, deliverance, and healing that the Lord has given to you.

Almighty Father, there are times when I feel trapped by medical "facts," and I feel my courage beginning to slip away. In my distress I call to You; from the depths of the waters I call for help. There are times when I feel my life is ebbing away like Jonah's. I raise my prayer to You, and I thank You for delivering me. It is written that Your Son, Jesus Christ, has taken my infirmities and borne my sicknesses. It is done. It is complete. So I raise my voice to You in joy, thanksgiving, and trust. In the name of Your Son, Jesus Christ, I pray, Amen.

✝

DAY 44
JESUS IS YOUR SECURE ROCK

And why call ye me, Lord, Lord, and do not the things which I say? Whosoever cometh to me, and heareth my sayings, and doeth them, I will show you to whom he is like:

He is a like a man which built an house, and digged deep, and laid the foundation on a rock: and when the flood arose, the stream beat vehemently upon that house, and could not shake it: for it was founded upon a rock.

But he that heareth, and doeth not, is like a man that without a foundation built an house upon the earth; against which the stream did beat vehemently, and immediately it fell; and the ruin of that house was great.   (Luke 6:46-49)

Not only must we speak words of belief but also we must put Jesus' words into practice. Saying that you put your faith and trust in God and in Christ Jesus means nothing if you are not willing to *live* your faith and trust every day.

We all know this is true intellectually, and most of us think we do live our faith. Yet when we feel sick, these words of Jesus become particularly relevant because we feel weak and vulnerable. Our ability to function is at a low ebb, and we sometimes are not thinking clearly. The evil one whispers in our ear, and we allow ourselves to be filled with fear.

We soon are faced with our moment of truth. Do we put the words of Jesus into action or not? What are Jesus' words? "Thou shalt love the Lord thy God with all thy heart, and with all thy soul, and with all thy mind" (Matthew 22:37). "Seek, and ye shall find" (Matthew 7:7). "What things soever ye desire, when ye pray, believe that ye receive them, and ye shall have them" (Mark 11:24).

When you feel sick, do you turn first to God for instruction about what you should do? Or do you turn first to humans? Do you look for spiritual roots of your problem, or do you assume your disease is only a physical matter? Do you follow God's instructions for each step of your treatment and healing? Or do you follow without question the treatment plans of humans?

How often it is that we follow our own course until something goes wrong, and then, after we find we have built a house without a foundation, we call on God to save us. Jesus asks us to build our house on Him from the beginning. Are you really willing to turn your life over to God?

Loving Father, teach me to trust You and to build my house only on You and Your Son, Jesus Christ, my Redeemer and Savior. You are the foundation that will never fail me. I trust You completely, and I will follow You every step of the way. In Jesus' name, I pray, Amen.

✝

DAY 45
THE PEACE OF GOD

Be careful for nothing; but in every thing by prayer and supplication with thanksgiving let your requests be made known unto God. And the peace of God, which passeth all understanding, shall keep your hearts and minds through Christ Jesus. (Philippians 4:6-7)

Worry depletes you and undermines your faith. But when you are attacked with an illness, there certainly seem to be endless opportunities for you to focus on your troubles. It is so easy to allow each new symptom to create a new concern that something else is going wrong. Too often, there is the looming fear that, if you take the wrong action, you will suffer a disastrous result, perhaps even death.

All of these fears and worries come from the enemy, who is the father of lies, but you cannot afford to entertain these fears for even one minute. The devil wants you to concentrate on your symptoms, and he is always happy to send you new ones. Let your spirit rise up and shout, "No! Jesus paid the price for my healing and no devil will steal it from me." In the name of Jesus and by the authority of Luke 10:19, take authority over the enemy, the fear, and the symptoms.

Renew your mind and cast out all fearful thoughts. Immerse yourself in the Word, which is the sure beacon of truth, encouragement, and faith. Let God make the final decisions in your healing process, and trust in the revelation knowledge given by the Holy Spirit.

Remember that having an attitude of gratitude is essential. As Paul says, present your requests to God "*with thanksgiving.*" Thank God for all the properly functioning parts of your body. Thank Him for guiding you to the right information about the underlying reason for your body's becoming so unbalanced as to be subject to the health condition you are experiencing. Thank God for being with you every step of the way, for guiding each decision, and for healing you.

What is the result of following this procedure in handling worry? The peace of God which passes all understanding. Peace in your heart. Peace in your soul. Peace in every cell in your body. And what better environment is there for healing?

Almighty God, I come to You in gratitude for the miracle of my body, which is the temple of the Holy Spirit. I give You all my worries about my health. I take charge of my thoughts and choose to replace every thought of worry with the positive promise of Your Word. I thank You, Father, for making my body whole through the blood of Jesus and I expect the physical manifestation of my healing so that everyone will see the evidence of Your great power and love. In Jesus' name, I pray, Amen.

✝

DAY 46
DO ALL THINGS WORK FOR YOUR GOOD?

And He Who searches the hearts of men knows what is in the mind of the [Holy] Spirit [what His intent is], because the Spirit intercedes and pleads [before God] in behalf of the saints according to and in harmony with God's will. We are assured and know that [God being a partner in their labor] all things work together and are [fitting into a plan] for good to and for those who love God and are called according to [His] design and purpose.
(Romans 8:27-28 Amplified Bible)

This statement of Paul that "all things work together for good" is often used to convince people that everything that happens to them is an act of God's will. Consequently, people don't resist satan and his destructive acts but actually declare them to be some mysterious act of God.

This confusion comes from removing the sentence from its context. Notice that Paul is talking about the effects of intercessory prayer which the Holy Spirit is making for the saints. Prayers are being offered by the Holy Spirit *according to and in harmony with God's will*. Nothing is being prayed for that is not according to God's will. We are now assured that, *whenever God is a partner*, all things work together for good for those who love Him. Wow! Now it all makes sense.

Do things happen to you that were *not* intended for your good? Absolutely, yes. Satan is not working for your good. Satan is trying to destroy you, to kill you, and to steal your health, finances, relationships, and joy. Attributing every event in your life to God is to deny satan's existence.

It is written that satan creeps around like a lion looking for prey. Some of the easiest pickings are those who believe that everything that happens in their life is planned by God. God has made it clear that people can *choose* between good and evil, between life and death, between Him and the devil. You have that choice a thousand times a day, and so does everyone else. God even tells you the answer: choose good, choose life, and choose Him.

The good news is that evil cannot win when we choose to follow the Lord God Almighty because Jesus has overcome satan. No matter how satan attacks you, no matter what illness or accident may befall you, the victory over it has already been won by Jesus Christ. God can create good out of any situation, no matter how badly it may have begun. Stand in the authority that God has given you and trust Him completely with your life.

Father, You know everything that I need. I ask the Holy Spirit to intercede for me in harmony with Your divine will. I am assured that, when You are my partner, all things coming from You work together for my good. Thank You, Father, for healing me. In Jesus' name, Amen.

✝

DAY 47
THE HOLY SPIRIT TEACHES YOU

But the Comforter, which is the Holy Ghost, whom the Father will send in my name, he shall teach you all things, and bring all things to your remembrance, whatsoever I have said unto you.
(John 14:26)

Jesus said, "The Holy Spirit will teach you all things." *All* things. "And he will remind you of all things I have said to you." *All* things.

What were those things? To love God with all our heart. To love one another. To heal the sick. To forgive one another. To forgive ourselves. To carry out His instructions with obedience and joy. To follow Him.

Jesus says that the Holy Spirit is going to help to continue His own work by reminding us constantly of everything He has said. One thing that Jesus said over and over again was that all things were possible. He warned those who were willing to hear Him not to be deceived by the appearance of things but instead to stand on faith and to believe that nothing is impossible. Then, just before He ascended into heaven, Jesus asked God to send us the Holy Spirit to remind us of this.

Sickness itself is a tool of the father of lies; so, when we feel ill, we are especially vulnerable to deceptive appearances and to "facts" that are really lying symptoms from the enemy. It is a major relief to know that we have been given a strong guide in the Holy Spirit to help us to find God's truth.

When we feel sick, we have an especially deep need for the Holy Spirit because the decisions we have to make are often literally life-and-death decisions. And there is no one single decision to be made. Instead, there are often hundreds of them as each day passes.

Just exactly how can the Holy Spirit guide us when we feel sick? By revealing to us the precise things we need to do at the exact moment that we ask. Sometimes we receive our healing all at once, but other times it is a gradual process. If our healing is a progressive one, the Holy Spirit can provide revelation knowledge to us to tell us nutrients we should eat, what herbs we should take, and what medical treatments we should follow. As we change and improve, the instructions that we receive will also change.

How wonderful to know that, when we are filled with the Holy Spirit, we are never without our teacher and our guide. With His help we are transformed, we are changed, and we are healed.

Almighty God, thank You for sending Your Holy Spirit to teach, instruct, and guide me. I am willing to listen to Him and to act on His instructions. I want to make decisions today that are the right ones for my recovery, and I am so grateful that You gave the Holy Spirit to me to help me choose wisely. In Jesus' name, I pray, Amen.

✝

DAY 48
DOES HEALING SURPRISE YOU?

...he (Peter) answered unto the people, Ye men of Israel, why marvel ye at this? or why look ye so earnestly on us, as though by our own power or holiness we had made this man to walk?

The God of Abraham, and of Isaac, and of Jacob, the God of our fathers, hath glorified his Son Jesus. ...

And his name through faith in his name hath made this man strong, whom ye see and know: yea, the faith which is by him hath given him this perfect soundness in the presence of you all. (Acts 3:12-13, 16)

Peter's question is one we need to ponder. Why *does* healing surprise us? From the first moment of the creation of mankind, we were made whole, well, and without sickness. Our willfulness caused us to know evil and to know disease, yet God never changed His desire. He reminds us in His Word that He is always our healer.

Because of His great love for us, He sent His Son to defeat the evil one and to take our illnesses on Himself through the stripes on His back. Yet here we are two thousand years later, just like the people in this story, still surprised by the power of God's healing hand.

How sad God must be that we have not comprehended what has already been done for us. Jesus has died for us, for our sins, and for our health. Matthew proclaims it. "Himself took our infirmities and bare our sicknesses" (Matthew 8:17). Peter proclaims it. "It is Jesus' name and the faith that comes through him that has given this perfect soundness to him." Hallelujah! It is written.

Stop being surprised. The members of the early church *expected* healing because they knew it was integral to Jesus' mission. Expect *your* healing to manifest. Read the entire chapter of Acts 3. Give the Word your attention. Give Jesus your attention.

Jesus told everyone that they must believe. Do it. It is the unbelievers who should be surprised, not the believers. Declare the Word several times a day, saying, "By faith in the name of Jesus, I am made strong. It is Jesus' name and the faith that comes through Him that gives me perfect soundness and complete healing."

Dear God, for too long I have been among those who are surprised by Your healing. No more. No more. I accept Your Son, Jesus Christ, as my Savior, my Healer, and my Deliverer. By faith in the name of Jesus, I am made strong. It is Jesus' name and the faith that comes through Him that gives me perfect soundness and complete healing. Help me to be a witness for You and an instrument for the healing of others. In the name of Jesus Christ, I pray, Amen.

✝

DAY 49
THE PROBLEM OF UNBELIEF

And Jesus said unto them, Because of your unbelief: for verily I say unto you, If ye have faith as a grain of mustard seed, ye shall say unto this mountain, Remove hence to yonder place; and it shall remove; and nothing shall be impossible unto you.
(Matthew 17:20)

Jesus' disciples had been healing the sick and casting out demons on a consistent basis by using the authority and power that Jesus had given them. Then they experienced what was apparently their first failure when they could not heal and deliver a man's son. Read the whole story in Matthew 17:14-21. You will see that Jesus was sharp with His disciples, expressing His displeasure that they had not been successful in carrying out His command to heal. He knew that there were no weaknesses or failures in His power, and He knew that He had delegated that power to the disciples.

After Jesus cast the demon out and healed the boy, the disciples came to Him with questions because they could not understand why they had failed. Notice that Jesus didn't tell them that they did not have enough faith.

Instead, He told them that unbelief was their problem. The Greek word for "faith" in this verse is *pistis*. The Greek word for "unbelief" is *apistia*. So we have faith and "not-faith," both at the same time. The Word makes it clear that God has given us our faith, so we surely have enough. What we are struggling with is the "not-faith," which is all the unbelief that we are carrying around.

Let's assume that you have two strong, healthy legs. If I put a chair in front of you, you are easily able to take a large step and stand up on the seat of the chair. Now let's imagine that you are standing in front of the chair with giant boots on that weigh 100 pounds each. Can you step up onto the seat of the chair now? Why not? Your legs are still strong and healthy. The problem isn't your legs; it's the 200 pounds of weight on your feet. Those weights are your unbelief.

Jesus repeatedly tells us that we have enough faith to accomplish the impossible. We don't really believe Him, though, and keep looking for more faith. Instead, what we need to do is to tear down the unbelief that hinders our faith. Once we are freed from the not-faith (the unbelief), then even a tiny mustard-seed-sized faith can work miracles.

Father God, I've been so focused on trying to get more faith, that I haven't paid much attention to all the areas of unbelief in my life. Now I know that all thoughts of unbelief are dangerous enemies to the effective release of my faith. Help me to root out the traditions of men that have embedded unbelief deep in my heart. Help me to remove all doubt so that I can exercise mountain-moving, disease-busting faith. In Jesus' name, I pray, Amen.

†

DAY 50
ROOT OUT UNBELIEF

He answereth him, and saith, O faithless generation, how long shall I be with you? How long shall I suffer you? Bring him unto me. ...

Jesus said unto him, If thou canst believe, all things are possible to him that believeth.

And straightway the father of the child cried out, and said with tears, Lord, I believe; help thou mine unbelief.
(Mark 9:19, 23-24)

Here is a second look at the story of the boy whom the disciples could not deliver and heal. In the version that Mark presents, we get a more distinct look at the simultaneous presence of belief and unbelief.

The boy's father cries out to Jesus, "Lord, I believe; help my unbelief!" Jesus does not reprimand the father or rebuke him for what he said. Instead, He receives it as truth that the man was in a state of belief and unbelief at the same time.

What are some of the major sources of your unbelief? Did you grow up in a church that taught you that God has a purpose in your being sick? Have you believed that God is punishing you? Or do you think that God is teaching you a lesson that you can't learn in any other way? Are you tormented by the doubt that God can heal other people but that you are somehow not worthy enough? Do you think that you don't pray enough or read your Bible enough to receive your healing?

Jesus makes it clear that it is your unbelief that stops your faith from working. Make a conscious decision to identify every thought of unbelief and tear it down. Replace each one with truth from the Word.

It is a lie from the enemy that you have to wait until you are "spiritual enough" before you can receive your healing. The fact is that you will never be spiritual enough on your own, just as you will never be worthy enough or righteous enough on your own.

Rejoice in the fact that you are righteous because you have the righteousness of Jesus and that is more than enough. Rejoice that you are worthy because you have the worthiness of Jesus and that is more than enough. Rejoice that you are spiritual because you have the Spirit of Jesus and that is more than enough.

Father God, I believe. Help thou my unbelief. Help me to root out every doubt and unbelief so that nothing hinders my faith from operating. Thank You for sending Your Son, Jesus, so that I am made righteous and worthy in Your sight through His shed blood. I declare joyously that I am blessed and that I am filled with divine health. In Jesus' name, I pray, Amen.

✝

DAY 51
DON'T BE DIVIDED AGAINST YOURSELF

And Jesus knew their thoughts, and said unto them, Every kingdom divided against itself is brought to desolation; and every city or house divided against itself shall not stand.   (Matthew 12:25)

All too often when we feel sick, we become divided against ourselves. Fighting "the disease" often ends up with our fighting parts of our own body. We even use terms of warfare when we talk about illness and the process to deal with it; for example, we speak of heart "attacks" as though our heart is attacking us.

Our body is never the enemy. It is a holy temple and God designed it to be healthy. Whenever we look at the cause of illness at the physical level, we generally find that the body part is not the culprit. For example, a gallbladder "attack" is the cry of an organ overwhelmed by years of improper eating. Cancer cells are our own cells, whose growth has gone wild and out of the pattern God designed for them, and they multiply because our immune system is too depleted to destroy them appropriately.

Your healing has already been provided. Think of television signals that are being transmitted twenty-four hours every day. If you can't see a program, it's not because the signals aren't being broadcast. It's because your set is either turned off or not working properly. Compare the healing power of God to those television signals. The twenty-four hour broadcasting began that day two thousand years ago when Jesus endured the stripes and the Cross. If you aren't receiving the flow of healing power, then something is interfering with your reception. Turn on your faith receptor. Look for areas of unbelief or other hindrances that are stopping the healing power that has already been released.

Put aside all thoughts of your body as your enemy so that you aren't divided against yourself. Do not let the enemy defeat you by getting you to fear or hate parts of your own body. Instead see every cell in your body through the Father's eyes as perfectly healthy and whole. For those cells that are out of control or are malfunctioning, command them to work properly in the name of Jesus. Command invading bacteria and viruses to leave, tumors to shrink, and blood pressure to be normal.

Rejoice, because by His stripes you were healed and are healed.

Dear gracious Father, help me to stop fighting myself. I know that the Holy Spirit dwells within me and that my body is His holy temple. Teach me to honor and respect it, to nourish and protect it. I command all spirits of infirmity to leave my body now. I stand on Your Holy Word in faith until I see the manifestation of total health in my temple. In Jesus' name, I pray, Amen.

✝

DAY 52
CAN YOU REALLY DO GREATER THINGS THAN JESUS?

I assure you, most solemnly I tell you, if anyone steadfastly believes in Me, he will himself be able to do the things that I do; and he will do even greater things than these, because I go to the Father. (John 14:12   Amplified Bible)

Most Christians say they believe Jesus and what He taught. Nevertheless, this Scripture usually makes most people take a deep breath and have second thoughts. The King James Version of this Scripture reads, "I say unto you, He that believeth on me, the works that I do shall he do also; and greater works than these shall he do; because I go unto my Father."

Jesus very plainly says that any person who believes in Him can do the things that He does. Not only that – but we are told we can do *greater* things than Jesus did because we will have His help as He sits at the right hand of the Father. His statement seemed so preposterous that He wanted to make sure we knew He wasn't joking. "Most solemnly I tell you," the Amplified Bible reads. "I tell you the truth," the New International Version reads. "Verily, verily," says the King James Version.

The Lord wants us to understand that, just as the Father was the source of all the works that He (Jesus) did while He was here on earth, the Father is the source of all works that we do. Jesus tells us that the Father will continue to do His mighty works by using us just as He used His Son.

God wanted His Son to teach, preach, and heal, so Jesus did exactly that. Jesus always did the works and the will of the Father. And Jesus taught His followers to do the same thing. God wants *us* to teach, preach, and heal. He wants you to be saved. He wants you to be healed. And He wants you to pass it on. Pass it on.

Jesus promises that we can pass it on in a way even greater than He passed it on when He was on earth. Why? Because we have His support as He has joined the Father. This is Christ's promise. Believe Him. And act on your belief.

Dear Heavenly Father, thank You for Your mighty works. Thank You for letting Your saving grace flow to me and around me. I accept Your Word and I want to serve You and to glorify You in everything that I do. Thank You for healing me – body, soul, mind, and emotions. Help me to be an example of Your glory, and help me to be a vessel for Your mighty works. Your Son, Jesus Christ, declared that I would do even greater works than He did. Use me, Father. Let Your power work in me for Your glory. In the name of Jesus Christ, I pray, Amen.

✝

DAY 53
DON'T GIVE UP!

And let us not be weary in well doing: for in due season we shall reap, if we faint not. (Galatians 6:9)

If Paul lived today and wanted to convey this message, he would probably say, "Hang in there! Don't give up, no matter what."

Have you prayed for your healing, but you haven't seen it manifested yet? Don't give up. Are you standing on the Word, but you don't see any improvement in the physical realm? Don't give up. Are you tired of feeling tired? Don't give up. Say it out loud three times: "I will not give up. I will not give up. I will not give up."

You *will* reap the harvest if you don't give up. If you are basing your belief that you are healed on seeing improvements in your symptoms, you are way off track. Faith is steadfast belief in what is *still unseen.* Remember that Paul exhorts us in 2 Corinthians 4:18 to "look not at the things which are seen, but at the things which are not seen: for the things which are seen are temporal; but the things which are not seen are eternal."

The biggest temptation is to let your negative feelings take control and determine your reality. "But I feel so bad," you may say. The Word tells us we must set our compass by the truth of the Word of God. We must be led by the

Lord, not by feelings that are not in agreement with the Word of God.

Satan wants you to quit, so he will use as many delaying tactics as he can. He will especially create lots of opportunity for doubts to creep in. Whenever he can get you to think, "maybe I won't be healed" or "since I don't see anything happening, maybe it really *is* God's will that I not get well," the evil one is claiming a victory. Erase those thoughts at once and replace them with God's truth found in His Word.

Never forget that Jesus Christ came to earth and gave His life for you. He took your infirmities to the Cross as well as your sins. It has already been done. Receive the victory of Jesus Christ. Read Holy Scripture, and notice how often Jesus told someone, "Your faith has made you whole." Over and over and over again He said it.

Do not lose faith. Take charge of your thoughts by replacing fear with faith, and root out every doubt. Claim the victory that Jesus Christ has won for *you*. Your healing will be manifested if you don't give up.

Wonderful Father God, thank You for giving me Your strength so that I won't become weary either in doing good or in standing on Your Word that declares that You are my healer. I apply the atoning blood of the Lord Jesus Christ to every organ and cell in my body, and I know that I will reap a harvest of recovery if I don't give up. In Jesus' name, I pray, Amen.

†

DAY 54
RISE AND WALK IN THE NAME OF JESUS

And a certain man lame from his mother's womb was carried, whom they laid daily at the gate of the temple which is called Beautiful, to ask alms of them that entered into the temple; who seeing Peter and John about to go into the temple asked an alms. And Peter, fastening his eyes upon him with John, said, Look on us. And he gave heed unto them, expecting to receive something of them.

Then Peter said, Silver and gold have I none; but such as I have give I thee: In the name of Jesus Christ of Nazareth rise up and walk. And he took him by the right hand, and lifted him up: and immediately his feet and ankle bones received strength. And he leaping up stood, and walked, and entered with them into the temple, walking, and leaping, and praising God. (Acts 3:2-8)

What is the church supposed to be like? In Acts you see the early church at work as the disciples followed the training that Jesus had given them. Basically Jesus gave them three instructions: to preach the gospel, to heal the sick, and to deliver those in bondage to the enemy.

As they go about fulfilling the mission that Jesus gave them, Peter and John encounter a man who had been crippled from birth. Suppose that man lived today. Imagine the size of the medical report on him. See in your mind all the scientific data showing that this man could never,

ever walk, and hear in your mind the words, "I'm sorry but nothing can be done."

The man asked Peter and John for money, but Peter told him, "Give me your attention, your full attention." The man did so, expecting to receive something. However, never in his wildest imagination did he expect to receive what he got, which was a complete healing.

Peter said, "Such as I have, I give you." What was it that he had? He had the Word ("it is written"), he had Jesus' example, he had Jesus' mission ("go ye ... and heal"), he had the power of the Holy Spirit, and he had faith.

You are not like the man at the temple gate who was without hope and just coping with his infirmity. Instead, you are like Peter and John, and you have the same power from the Holy Spirit in you that they did. You must understand that fact and believe it in the very core of your being.

Give God your full attention, and expect to receive His love, blessings, and healing. Declare positive words of your faith daily. In the name of Jesus Christ of Nazareth, your Redeemer, walk in health.

Dear God, thank You for showing me how the first followers of Your Son, Jesus Christ, fulfilled the mission to heal the sick. I look to You and Your Son and give You my full attention. I focus in expectation and belief. I gratefully receive Your healing and Your blessings so that I may glorify Your Holy name. In the name of Jesus Christ, my Redeemer, I pray, Amen.

†

Day 55
Be Careful What You Think

Finally, brethren, whatsoever things are true, whatsoever things are honest, whatsoever things are just, whatsoever things are pure, whatsoever things are lovely, whatsoever things are of good report; if there be any virtue, and if there be any praise, think on these things.

Those things, which ye have both learned, and received, and heard, and seen in me, do: and the God of peace shall be with you.
(Philippians 4:8-9)

Whatever you spend your time thinking about reveals the condition of your innermost heart and spirit. That is a rather sobering thought, isn't it? Particularly when we apply it to our health.

Do you spend your day thinking about God's truth that He has paid the price for your healing? Do you spend your day repeating God's healing promises? Do you spend your day giving thanks to God for healing you? Do you spend your day listening for the Holy Spirit to reveal to you ways that you can promote your good health? Do you spend your day creating pictures in your mind of yourself living whole and healthy? Do you spend your day repeating to God your trust that He is your Great Physician?

Or do you spend your day listening to the father of lies tell you that God's will is to bring sickness on earth? Do you spend your day following the advice of family, friends, and medical personnel without having received divine guidance and instructions first? Do you spend your day thinking about this pain or that discomfort? Do you spend your day creating pictures in your mind of yourself getting worse? Do you spend your day preparing for degeneration in your condition because it has been predicted for your illness? Do you spend your day planning your funeral?

Whatever you think defines who you really are and what you will become. Think on positive things and join with your Creator to bring them into reality. This is positive thinking produced by *speaking God's own Words back to Him.* It is not just mindless repetition of positive affirmations, and it is not just wishful thinking which attempts to override human doubt. God's positive Word reinforces your faith, and it is your faith which makes you whole.

Almighty God, I fill myself with Your Holy Word. I choose to listen to You and fill my mind with Your Holy Scripture and with hymns of praise. I will think on those things that are true, honest, just, pure, lovely, and especially those things that are of good report. I rejoice that You have given me a good report, and I see every doctor's report stamped with Your own verdict, "Totally healed by a miracle of God!" In the name of Christ Jesus, my Redeemer, I pray, Amen.

†

Day 56
Hope Means Expectation

Now the God of hope fill you with all joy and peace in believing, that ye may abound in hope, through the power of the Holy Ghost. (Romans 15:13)

Paul describes God as the "God of hope." Sometimes the English meaning of words is a little misleading and that is true here. In English, when we say we are "hoping" for something, we are not sure whether it will happen or not. Thus, in our minds hoping and wishing are somewhat similar. People hope that they will win the lottery and have no actual belief that it is likely to happen at all. They are just hoping.

Although Paul speaks of hope, he also uses the phrase, "as you trust in him." Trust is based on a definite belief in something or someone and does not include uncertainty. Trust between two people has to be developed slowly to allow a time of testing to see if each party will be faithful to his word. To hope that you will keep your word and to trust that you will keep your word are two very different things.

Let's look at the Greek to see what Paul is really saying here in Romans. The word translated "hope" in the King James Version is *elpis*, which means expectation, confidence, faith, and hope. Now we have something totally different, don't we? "Now the God of expectation and confidence and faith and hope fill you with all joy and peace in believing, that you may abound in expectation, confidence, faith, and hope through the power of the Holy Ghost." Wow!

Father God is the God of His Word. When you stand on God's Word, you do more than hope. You expect God to fulfill His Word. You do not wonder if He will or wonder if He can or guess whether He wants to help you. You *know*. You believe. You trust. You have confidence.

With confidence we look beyond appearances and see our challenges through the eyes of God. We are bolstered and lifted to declare that "I can do all things through Christ who strengthens me." We are bold to stand on God's Word that He is the God who heals us. We are filled with the knowledge that nothing is too hard for God and that He reigns supreme over everything and everyone, including the evil one.

Be filled with the spirit of the Lord. Let your life radiate the joy and peace of knowing that God keeps His Word.

Father God, thank You for filling me with Your Holy Spirit so that I overflow with Your confidence and expectation. I proclaim with absolute trust that You keep Your Word. You have declared Yourself as the God who heals me. I receive that truth into the depths of my heart. I believe, Father, and am filled with joy and peace. In Jesus' name, I pray, Amen.

†

Day 57
Keep Scriptures in Front of You

My son, attend to my words; incline thine ear unto my sayings.
Let them not depart from thine eyes; keep them in the midst of
thine heart. For they are life unto those that find them, and health
to all their flesh.   (Proverbs 4:20-22)

These three verses in Proverbs sum up some of the most
important steps for being healed. Look at the first sentence:
"My son, attend to my words; incline thine ear unto my
sayings." Attend means "to pay attention." God is saying,
"Pay attention. Pay attention to My words. Listen to what I
have to tell you."

And how do you do that? By studying His Word written
in the Holy Scripture and also by listening to His voice as
He gives you revelation knowledge. If you want to receive
your healing, then search out passages in the Bible that
speak of God's will on the subject. Fill your mind, heart,
and soul with God's Word. You will find many of them in
this little book, but there are hundreds more.

Certain verses of Scripture will touch your heart more
than others. Write them down on note cards and post
them around the house on your bathroom mirror, on the
refrigerator door, or on the end table next to your favorite
chair.

Another way to fill your mind and spirit with the Word of God is to get some CDs or downloads of the New Testament. Play them when you are in the car, while you are doing housework, and when you are taking some quiet time to rest and relax.

You may also want to make your own recording of the passages of Scripture that are especially powerful for you. Listening to your own voice speaking God's Words of healing and love is very empowering.

Begin to memorize healing verses, and say them to yourself as often as possible during the day. Incline your ear to the sayings of the Lord. God wants your full attention as though you were straining to hear something being whispered to you. God tells you in His Word what He has done for you. He tells you that you were healed by the stripes of Jesus. Be diligent and faithful to find these mighty messages from your Lord and Healer.

Wonderful Father God, how grateful I am to have Your Holy Scripture to lift me and strengthen me. Give me the discipline to incline my ears more often to Your sayings. Help me to develop habits of immersing myself in Your Word, and help me to listen to Your Holy voice. Your words are, indeed, both life to me and health to my flesh. Thank You, Father, for Your faithful, loving guidance. In the name of Jesus Christ, I pray, Amen.

†

Day 58
What Do You Want from Jesus?

... and as he went out of Jericho with his disciples and a great number of people, blind Bartimaeus, the son of Timaeus, sat by the highway side begging. And when he heard that it was Jesus of Nazareth, he began to cry out, and say, Jesus, thou son of David, have mercy on me.

And many charged [warned] him that he should hold his peace: but he cried the more a great deal, Thou son of David, have mercy on me. And Jesus stood still, and commanded him to be called. And they call the blind man, saying unto him, Be of good comfort, rise; he calleth thee. And he ... rose, and came to Jesus.

And Jesus answered and said unto him, What wilt thou that I should do unto thee? The blind man said unto him, Lord, that I might receive my sight.

And Jesus said unto him, Go thy way; thy faith hath made thee whole. And immediately he received his sight, and followed Jesus in the way. (Mark 10:46-52)

Why would Jesus ask a blind man, "What do you want me to do for you"? Surely He knew Bartimaeus wanted his sight to be restored. Yet Jesus still asked him what he wanted.

Notice that Bartimaeus had been extremely persistent in getting Jesus' attention. He kept calling out, even though those around him told him to be quiet. Jesus valued persistence so He stopped and gave Bartimaeus His complete focus. Then the Lord wanted to know the man's true intent. Bartimaeus answered quickly and without hesitation, "I want to see." Jesus' reply was just as swift, "Go your way; your faith has made you whole."

Notice that Jesus didn't just heal his eyes, but he made Bartimaeus whole. We find the Greek word "*sozo*" again. "Go your way," Jesus says. "Your faith has '*sozo*-ed' you – saved you, healed you, delivered you, and made you whole."

Today Jesus turns to you and asks, "What do you want Me to do for you?" Do you want to be made whole? Or do you just want your symptoms to go away so that you can keep doing everything you've been doing? Are you looking for relief without responsibility?

Answer the Lord with honesty, willingness, intention, and faith, and then receive your healing.

Merciful God, I put myself in the place of Bartimaeus saying, Lord, I want to be well. And, Lord, I really do want to be following the plan You have for my life. I'm ready to stop doing everything my way, and instead, I surrender my life to You and truly yield to Your plan. I thank You that Your Word to me is rapid and clear, "Go your way. Your faith has healed you and made you whole." I stand on this precious Scripture and see with my spiritual eyes that by the stripes of Jesus I am indeed healed. In the mighty name of Jesus, my Lord and Savior, I pray, Amen.

✝

Day 59
Choose Life

I call heaven and earth to record this day against you, that I have set before you life and death, blessing and cursing: therefore choose life, that both thou and thy seed may live:

That thou mayest love the Lord thy God, and that thou mayest obey his voice, and that thou mayest cleave unto him: for he is thy life, and the length of thy days: that thou mayest dwell in the land which the Lord sware unto thy fathers, to Abraham, to Isaac, and to Jacob, to give them. (Deuteronomy 30:19-20)

God gives you free will. He sets before you the power to choose what you want - life or death, blessings or curses. And He urges you to choose Him, to choose life.

This Scripture tells us what flows from choosing life: you will live, love the Lord your God, obey His voice, and hold fast to Him. God is very aware that every moment in the day presents you with choices. Most are tiny choices, but they are choices nevertheless. When you choose life, you proclaim your love of God. And when you choose life, you depend on God's guidance by listening to His voice and obeying.

Each morning when you wake up, say "thank you" to God and consciously choose life for the new day. If you feel sick, this can sometimes seem difficult. There are some mornings when you wake up feeling tired before the day has even begun. The hours that stretch before you seem long, and a spirit of fatigue tries to lead you into feelings of despair.

It is at these moments that it is critical to choose life. Remember, when God is in your cheering section, who can defeat you? The Lord *is* your life, so to choose life is to choose God.

Also choose to accept your responsibility to take the authority that Jesus died to give you. He told you in Luke 10:19 that you have power over all the power of the enemy. So, in the name of Jesus, command all spirits of discouragement and all spirits of infirmity to leave you. Do not play victim to the evil one who wants to kill you.

Jesus has won the victory for you. He gives you life abundant. Choose me, He says. Choose life.

Almighty God, I boldly proclaim that I choose life. I choose life, God! I shout it with all of my might. I love You, my Creator. Jesus gave me life abundant and I receive! I receive it! I am excited, Father God, by the future. I am excited to share with others and to let them know that Jesus has purchased their salvation, deliverance, and healing. Help me to fulfill Your mission and Your purpose for me on this earth, Father. In the name of Your Son, Jesus Christ, my Savior and my Redeemer, I pray, Amen.

✝

DAY 60
BE RESTORED

And when he was departed thence, he went into their synagogue: And, behold, there was a man which had his hand withered. And they asked him, saying, Is it lawful to heal on the sabbath days? that they might accuse him.

And he said unto them, What man shall there be among you, that shall have one sheep, and if it fall into a pit on the sabbath day, will he not lay hold on it, and lift it out? How much then is a man better than a sheep? Wherefore it is lawful to do well on the sabbath days. Then saith he to the man, Stretch forth thine hand. And he stretched it forth; and it was restored whole, like as the other. (Matthew 12:9-13)

This story from Matthew emphasizes the importance that God places on saving His people and on healing them. When Jesus is challenged with the question of the legality of healing on the Sabbath, He gives an illustration of a shepherd who saves a sheep that has fallen into a pit on the Sabbath Day. He continues by asking, "How much then is a man better than a sheep?"

Standing before Him on a Sabbath day is a man with a withered hand. Jesus demonstrates that the real issue doesn't have to do with rabbinical law. It has to do with the importance that God places on meeting the needs of His children. The Son of God is very clear that it is always God's will for His children to be rescued.

In this particular instance, how does Jesus perform the healing? He tells the man to take action. This is an action of faith in advance of any manifestation of healing. "Stretch forth thine hand," He says. The man believed, followed the instruction that he was given, and was healed.

God is your Good Shepherd. He cares for you and has sent His Son to rescue you from the pit of sickness and disease. It has already been done. Jesus came and He took your infirmities and bore your sicknesses on the Cross.

He has also sent the Holy Spirit as the beacon of truth to guide you and to reveal to you what action you are to take. Over and over again, God tells you that He has a plan for you and that it is a plan for good. Jehovah watches over you as a shepherd guards his sheep - protecting, healing, and saving you.

Father God, I have been like one of the little sheep who fell into the pit. Thank You for rescuing me, saving me, delivering me, and healing me. Thank You for Your constant and tender care and Your abiding love. I know that I can trust You because You are always faithful. I love Your Holy Word, and I meditate on it to plant seeds of truth in my heart every day. Thank You, Father, for Your goodness and mercy. In Jesus' mighty name, I pray, Amen.

†

DAY 61
YOU ARE AS YOU THINK IN YOUR HEART

For as he thinketh in his heart, so is he.   (Proverbs 23:7)

Of all the sentences in Holy Scripture, this is one of the most profound ones. Our thoughts lead to our actions and thus we create our experience and our world. Although there are people who do not think that God exists, Christians have a relationship with God that is very real and very powerful. The thoughts of the atheist don't make God disappear, but they do change the way the atheist interprets everything in his life.

The same thing is true about illness. If we think that disease is defined solely by medical tests, then we cannot reach to the level where faith is the *substance* and *evidence* of things *unseen*. If we think that God made us sick, we are placed in a position of conflict to ask Him to heal us. If we think that we are being made ill in order for us to learn a lesson, we have an internal confusion over being well.

Most of us give medical reports great power. Occasionally, the conclusion of the report is that we have a condition for which there is no current medical cure. Usually there are medical treatments available, but almost all of them carry serious risks and cause severe side effects.

The problem comes when we limit our thinking to these possibilities and *only* these possibilities. We allow our thinking to be controlled by medical authorities instead of praying with our doctors and putting the final decision in the hands of the Great Physician. As a man thinketh, so is he. If you think all healing must involve medical intervention, then so it is. If you think all medical opinions must be followed, then so it is.

On the other hand, if you think the Great Physician can guide and advise you about which medical treatments to take or not to take, then so it is. If you think that God wants you to be well, then so it is. If you think Jesus bore all your illnesses on the Cross, then so it is. If you think you are healed and the manifestation is happening now, then so it is.

God's Word confirms all these things. Believe them with your whole heart and declare that you are the way God sees you – healed and whole.

Dear God, too often I find myself thinking things that I know don't line up with Your Word. Therefore, I now make a conscious decision to change my thoughts. Faith comes by hearing and hearing by the Word of God, so I choose to fill my mind with Scriptures from Your Holy Word. I focus my thoughts on You, Father, and trust in Your will, Your guidance, and Your healing grace. In Jesus' mighty name, I pray, Amen.

†

Day 62
The Blessing of Communion

... That the Lord Jesus the same night in which he was betrayed took bread: And when he had given thanks, he brake it, and said, Take, eat: this is my body, which is broken for you: this do in remembrance of me.

After the same manner also he took the cup, when he had supped, saying, This cup is the new testament in my blood: this do ye, as oft as ye drink it, in remembrance of me.   *(1 Corinthians 11:23-25)*

Jesus established the ordinance that we call the Lord's Supper. Sharing it with others is a very special time for Christians, for it brings us close to each other and to our Lord Jesus Christ.

Notice that we partake of both bread and wine. Why two items? If Jesus wanted us to remember Him, we would need only one. Perhaps two items were important because there were two parts to His mission and there were also two parts to His sacrificial death. It is written that Jesus bore our sins *and* our infirmities on the Cross. Therefore, Jesus gave us the two separate elements in the Lord's Supper to remind us.

"... he ... took bread: And when he had given thanks, he brake it, and said, Take, eat: this is my body, which is broken for you." He took our infirmities so we eat the bread in remembrance of His body which was broken for us. "By His stripes we were healed" (1 Peter 2:24).

We eat the bread in remembrance that "the life also of Jesus might be made manifest in our mortal flesh" (2 Corinthians 4:11). We are to live fully and healthily in this body in complete service to the Lord God Almighty until we have fulfilled our days and the Lord takes us to be with Him forever.

When Jesus took the cup, He said, "This ...is the new testament in my blood." What does "the new testament" mean? It represented salvation, the redemption of our eternal spirit and the forgiveness of sins. It represented deliverance from demonic powers. It represented freedom from the bondage of poverty. And it once again represented the healing of our bodies. The cup represented the fullness of everything that the Greek word "*sozo*" means.

Celebrate the Lord's Supper with special thanksgiving, knowing that Jesus was the perfect Atonement for you – body, soul, and spirit.

Father God, thank You for the sacrifice of Your Son, Jesus Christ, who died on the Cross for me. For me. He bore my sins and He bore my infirmities. I eat the bread and am not afraid to live, fulfilling Your purpose for me on this earth. And I drink the cup and am not afraid to die, passing into life eternal. In Jesus' name, I pray, Amen.

†

DAY 63
BE MADE WHOLE

And as he entered into a certain village, there met him ten men that were lepers, which stood afar off: And they lifted up their voices, and said, Jesus, Master, have mercy on us.

And when he saw them, he said unto them, Go shew yourselves unto the priests. And it came to pass, that, as they went, they were cleansed.

And one of them, when he saw that he was healed, turned back, and with a loud voice glorified God. And fell down on his face at his feet, giving him thanks: and he was a Samaritan. And Jesus answering said, Were there not ten cleansed? but where are the nine? There are not found that returned to give glory to God, save this stranger.

And he said unto him, Arise, go thy way: thy faith hath made thee whole. (Luke 17:12-19)

Ten lepers cried out to Jesus for mercy. Jesus responded by telling them to go to the priests, who were required by Levitical law to determine if someone had been healed. We can assume from the story that the men did not see their healing manifested at the moment that Jesus spoke to them. Therefore, it would have required a step of faith to start out to the priests even though they had not seen any change in their condition.

Scripture says that all ten men were healed *as they went* on their way. They moved out in faith and then the healing was manifested. Sometimes we, too, receive our recovery as the product of a journey to wellness rather than as the result of an instantaneous miracle. It may be slower, but it is no less of a healing.

All ten men were cleansed of leprosy, but pay attention to this: only one man was pronounced whole by Jesus. Our Savior had cleansed them all at the same time and in the same way. Only the Samaritan came back to say "thank you" and only this one man was considered by Jesus to be made whole!

If you look in your concordance, you will see that the Greek word for "made whole" is "*sozo.*" This Scripture says that only one man received the whole package of being made whole. Since leprosy often resulted in people losing fingers or toes, don't you think "being made whole" would include the restoration of those missing body parts?

The issue of gratitude was the main point of this account of healing; however, we will focus on the concept of wholeness. Too often we confuse the disappearance of symptoms with being well. Being well is returning to the wholeness of body, mind, emotions, and soul that God intended. It means far more than not having lesions of leprosy on your body or a consumptive cough or a growing tumor. It includes those things, but it is more than those things.

It is particularly easy today to go for the "quick fix." We buy into the illusion that, if we can make a symptom go away, we have solved the problem. We want to make no changes in our choices or behavior, and we take no responsibility for the spiritual roots or the demonic influences that are involved. Thus, we almost guarantee that we will be sick again. And we are too foolish to see the connection. In fact, we usually insist that there is none.

Do you want to feel better momentarily? Or do you want to be truly well and whole? Are you expressing your gratitude and saying thank you right now? Or are you waiting until you are totally well? Adopt an attitude of gratitude that will keep you close to God. It will keep you receptive to hearing God's will for you, and it will keep you willing to follow that guidance with active choices for healing in your life.

View your recovery from the perspective of constant gratitude. Offer your thanks no matter what the appearance is about the state of your healing. Remember, Jesus said "thank You" to God for hearing Him before He ever called Lazarus forth from the grave. Right now, say out loud, "Thank You, God, for healing me." Receive His healing power.

Merciful God, I come with a grateful heart saying, "Thank You, thank You." It is my desire to come before You always in praise, adoration, and thanksgiving. I hear Jesus say directly to me, "Get up. Go your way. Your faith has made you whole." Father, I will sing my song of thanksgiving to You, glorifying Your name as long as I live. In Jesus' name, I pray, Amen.

†

Day 64
Power Over All the Power
of the Enemy

And he said unto them, I beheld Satan as lightning fall from heaven. Behold, I give unto you power to tread on serpents and scorpions, and over all the power of the enemy: and nothing shall by any means hurt you.

Notwithstanding in this rejoice not, that the spirits are subject unto you; but rather rejoice, because your names are written in heaven. (Luke 10:18-20)

Jesus is eternal. He was with the Father from before the beginning, and He was present before Lucifer ever became satan. Here in Luke we hear Jesus telling us that He was present when satan was cast out from heaven, and we know that Jesus will be here after satan has been put away forever.

Satan was only an angel. He was never divine and never will be so – even though what he seeks is our worship, or at the very least, our fear.

Now look at the next words, "I give unto you power [authority] to tread on serpents and scorpions, and over all the power of the enemy: and nothing shall by any means hurt you." Who is Jesus talking to? In this text, He is talking to the seventy missionaries that He is sending out to heal the sick, to deliver those oppressed by the evil one, and to preach the gospel that the kingdom of God is near. Did these people have any special skills for such a mission? Not in the beginning. However, after they were commissioned and equipped by Jesus, they walked in miracle-working power.

We are just like those seventy missionaries. Jesus has given every believer the same command to do His works, and He has equipped us, just as He equipped those first followers.

"I give unto you power [authority]," He says. What does this mean? It means that you can use the name of Jesus just as though He were here in the flesh. It means that you can call on Him anytime to act in accordance with the will of God. Who do you have authority over? Satan. You have authority in the name of Jesus to trample on the evil one and to overcome anything the evil one sends your way. That includes sickness and disease.

Enforce the authority that Christ has given to you. Command every spirit of infirmity to leave you in the name of Jesus and speak health and wholeness over every cell in your body. Proclaim the healing of Jehovah-Rapha, the God who heals you.

Father God, it is written that I have been given authority to overcome all the power of the enemy. No power is stronger than Yours. Nothing will harm me. In the name of Jesus, I bind every attack of the evil one, and I command every spirit of infirmity to leave my body. Father, I declare that I am healed and victorious in the mighty name of Jesus, in whose name I pray, Amen.

†

DAY 65
THE BIBLE IS GOD'S INSPIRED WORD

All Scripture is given by inspiration of God, and is profitable for doctrine, for reproof, for correction, for instruction in righteousness:

That the man of God may be perfect, thoroughly furnished unto all good works.   (2 Timothy 3:16-17)

What is our best teacher and the best source for help, for encouragement, and for examples? The Holy Scripture. God wants us to use His Holy Word as our guide because it marks the way for us. In the New International Version of this letter written to Timothy, Paul describes Holy Scripture as "God-breathed." Isn't that a beautiful way to express the fact that it is divinely inspired? Through it, God's voice rings out clear and true.

It is vital to turn to God's Word when you feel ill or have been injured. The Bible is your beacon, lighting the way for you. It teaches you God's truth and God's good news – that He is the God who heals you and that Jesus Christ bore your sins and infirmities on the Cross for you.

It also instructs, corrects, and trains you. God does not teach you by making you sick. He teaches you through His Holy Word. The Bible teaches you how to pray. It teaches you how to live. It teaches you healthy foods to eat. It teaches you how to ask for healing. It teaches you about repentance and deliverance. It teaches you the importance of asking the Holy Spirit for guidance. It teaches you how to trust.

Being filled with illustrations of men and women who sought God, as well as those who rejected God, it trains you by example. It shows you the lessons of Jonah, Job, Hezekiah, and Ezekiel. It shows you the example of His Son, Jesus Christ.

It even rebukes you and shows you the consequences of your actions. It shows you the results of failing to forgive others. It shows you the results of immoral physical activities on your body. It shows you the results of tempting God by willfully doing something harmful to your body and then asking for protection and healing.

One of our most magnificent blessings is to have Holy Scripture as our personal teacher. Turn to God's Word, and hear the Lord God Almighty speak to you.

Dear God, thank You for giving me Your Holy Word as my teacher and my guide. Today I take the time to explore Your Word and to ponder on its meaning for me in my life. Guide me to the lessons in it that will be most helpful for me today. Thank You. In Jesus' name, I pray, Amen.

†

DAY 66
JESUS AND THE FATHER ARE ONE

If I do not the works of my Father, believe me not. But if I do, though ye believe not me, believe the works: that ye may know, and believe, that the Father is in me, and I in him. (John 10:37-38)

Jesus answered them, I told you, and ye believed not: the works that I do in my Father's name, they bear witness of me. But ye believe not, because ye are not of my sheep, as I said unto you.

My sheep hear my voice, and I know them, and they follow me: and I give unto them eternal life; and they shall never perish, neither shall any man pluck them out of my hand. My Father, which gave them me, is greater than all; and no man is able to pluck them out of my Father's hand. I and my Father are one. (John 10:25-30)

Philip said to Him, Lord, show us the Father [cause us to see the Father – that is all we ask]; then we shall be satisfied. Jesus replied, Have I been with all of you for so long a time, and do you not recognize and know Me yet, Philip? Anyone who has seen Me has seen the Father. How can you say then, Show us the Father? Do you not believe that I am in the Father, and that the Father is in Me?

What I am telling you I do not say on My own authority and of My own accord; but the Father Who lives continually in Me does the (His) works (His own miracles, deeds of power). Believe Me that I am in the Father and the Father in Me; or else believe Me for the sake of the [very] works themselves. [If you cannot trust

Me, at least let these works that I do in My Father's name convince you.] (John 14:8-11 Amplified Version)

"I and my Father are one," Jesus said. "If I don't do the works of my Father, don't believe me." Jesus plainly tells us not to believe Him unless He is doing the works of the Father. He couldn't make it any clearer.

Surely He must have gotten tired of saying the same thing hundreds of times. "Look at what I am doing. I don't do a single thing that I don't see my Father doing. I don't do a single thing that my Father doesn't want Me to do. I am always working my Father's will. If you look at Me, you will see the Father. We are one. We are one."

Doesn't this lift your heart and make your spirit soar? With this truth you ought to feel the strength of the Lord flood through your whole body and give you new resolve to reach out to embrace the Living Word.

Jesus healed every single person who came to Him to be made well. He expelled demons from those who were op- presssed. And He said that these works bore witness that He was operating in His Father's name. He never made anyone sick to teach them an important life lesson. He never refused to heal anyone – not one single time.

Let the works of Jesus convince you that God wants you to be well. Jesus Himself pleads with you to do this. Listen to Him. Believe Him.

Give thanks that Jesus has already paid the price for you – spirit, soul, and body. It is written. Enforce the words of Jesus on every cell in your body, and tell each organ to function normally. Declare your concentrated, focused faith and believe in your healing.

Father God, I believe You. I believe Your Son. He came, and He did Your works to carry out Your will and to display Your glory to everyone around Him. I hear His voice, and I choose to obey His commands. Thank You, Father, for teaching me. Thank You for saving me. Thank You for healing me. Thank You, Father, for Your great love for me. I love You, Father. I love You. In Jesus' name, I pray, Amen.

†

DAY 67
GOD KEEPS HIS COVENANT

For all the promises of God in him are yea, and in him Amen, unto the glory of God by us.   (2 Corinthians 1:20)

My covenant will I not break, nor alter the thing that is gone out of my lips. (Psalm 89:34)

Cast not away therefore your confidence, which hath great recompense of reward. For ye have need of patience, that, after ye have done the will of God, ye might receive the promise. (Hebrews 10:35-36)

For we walk by faith, not by sight.   (2 Corinthians 5:7)

While we look not at the things which are seen, but at the things which are not seen: for the things which are seen are temporal; but the things which are not seen are eternal.   (2 Corinthians 4:18)

God has an answer for every promise He has made. It's "yes, yes, yes!" Father God tells us that He will not break any covenant He has made with us, and He will not change His mind.

If He has declared that we are healed by the stripes of Jesus, God will not suddenly decide that that promise isn't good on Wednesday or that it applies to everyone except you. If He has declared that Jesus took our sicknesses, God will not decide that is true for most illnesses except cancer. We can stand with confidence on God's Word precisely because it is *God's* Word. He does not lie, and He always does what He says He will do. We will receive every promise if we do not get distracted by deception and lies from the enemy and if we will not waver.

We have to walk by faith instead of by what we see. We have to keep our eyes focused on Jesus and on the finished work of the Cross. The things that we see are only physical. God is a spirit and acts in the spirit realm. The manifestation of what He does in the spirit realm is largely up to us and to our exercising our faith to trust God.

Father God, I praise You and give You all the glory that You have declared that Your answer to every promise is yes! I trust that You are the same yesterday, today, and forever and that You will never break Your covenant with me. I choose to walk by faith and not by sight. I choose to look at the spiritual, eternal things that are not seen rather than the temporal things that I see in the physical realm. I hold to my confidence in You, Father. I love You. In Jesus' name, I pray, Amen.

†

DAY 68
JESUS HEALED THEM ALL

... and great multitudes followed him, and he healed them all. (Matthew 12:15)

We so often hear people and ministers say that it is "God's will" that a certain individual be sick. Sometimes there is the suggestion that illness makes people strong or noble. Sometimes there is the suggestion that the illness is meant to teach us a lesson. Sometimes sickness is believed to be a way that God punishes people who have been "bad."

If you believe any of these ideas, then you can't be sure if God desires to heal *you*. You have little on which to build your faith. Keep your focus on the places where God's will is clear – first, in heaven where His will is kept perfectly and, second, in the life and mission of His Son, Jesus Christ. "I do nothing of myself," Jesus said in John 8:28.

In today's passage in Matthew 12, Jesus once again healed *all* who sought Him. He healed everyone in the great multitudes. No illness was excluded and no person was excluded. If it weren't God's will that *all* be healed, Jesus would not have healed everyone.

Surely, He would have said to some, "I'm sorry, but God is trying to teach you an important lesson, and I can't violate the will of the Father. So I can't heal you, but I will pray that you understand the lesson." He would have had to say that on many, many occasions, and certainly it would have been reported at least *once* in Scripture. However, no matter what translation you read, you will never find Jesus refusing to heal. Never. Notice how consistently Jesus healed *all* who came to Him.

Since Jesus was always acting on the will of God and since Jesus healed them *all*, it must be the will of God for all to be healed. That includes you. It is really critical that you receive this truth in your heart. Close your eyes and stand before Jesus, your Savior and Redeemer. See Him look at you, smile, forgive your sins, and heal you with His touch.

Dear God, thank You for the example of Your Son, Jesus Christ, who came to carry out Your will and to heal those who came to Him. I come before You as one of Your children. I ask forgiveness for my sins, and I declare Your will for my healing as revealed in Holy Scripture. I stand before You in trust and acceptance for Your personal love for me. Thank You for healing me, Father. In the name of Jesus Christ, I pray, Amen.

✝

DAY 69
FREELY GIVE WHAT YOU HAVE RECEIVED

... freely ye have received, freely give.   (Matthew 10:8)

Pass it on! Pass it on! These are Jesus' words with an important message. We are to pass on what we have received. And what is it that we have received? The answer is in the sentence just before this one: "And as ye go, preach, saying, The kingdom of heaven is at hand. Heal the sick, cleanse the lepers, raise the dead, cast out devils" (Matthew 10:7-8). Incredible! Jesus' definition of discipleship includes salvation, healing, deliverance, and wholeness. We have received all these gifts from the Lord, and we are to pass them on.

What an awesome message! Jesus gives to us freely. And He Himself is doing just as He is telling us here in Matthew to do. Jesus Himself freely receives from the Father, and He freely passes it on to others as the Father wishes Him to do. Yesterday, today, and forever.

God is a personal God. He desires an intimate relationship with each one of us. From the beginning He created a garden where He could walk personally with each of His children. He has always wanted this and He has never changed. When Adam and Eve made the disastrous choice to disobey Him, God found a way to redeem us.

This redemptive message of salvation, healing, deliverance, and being made whole is a glorious one. It is a message of our complete restoration – spirit, soul, and body. God needs us to spread this message. Each person who receives all these marvelous benefits must pass them on to someone else. We have to let people know that God wants them to be well. We have to form a chain of love with each person passing on what he or she has received.

One by one we stand linked together, and each one of us then becomes stronger than we could ever be on our own. Our healing magnifies as we stand together linked to our Lord.

Father God, thank You for Your abundant mercies. Thank You for my healing. Help me to be a witness to others of Your grace, Your love, and Your healing power. Many people are hurting today, and they don't know about Your message of wholeness. Use me according to Your plan for me and for others. I am willing to follow the directions of Your Son who said, "Freely ye have received, freely give." Guide me always. In Jesus' name, I pray, Amen.

✝

DAY 70
ARISE AND WALK IN VICTORY

For, lo, the winter is past, the rain is over and gone; the flowers appear on the earth; the time of the singing of birds is come, and the voice of the turtle is heard in our land; the fig tree putteth forth her green figs, and the vines with the tender grape give a good smell. Arise, my love, my fair one, and come away. (Song of Solomon 2:11-13)

This beautiful Song of Solomon beckons you forward into the present and away from the past. Leave behind the winter of old beliefs that held you prisoner. Leave behind the rains of doubt that kept you trapped in your illness.

God calls to you, "Come away, my beloved child. Come away. I have provided life, victory, health, and wholeness for you." Every day explore the Word of God and look at it with fresh eyes, asking for revelation knowledge from the Holy Spirit who resides within you. You will know the truth and it will make you free.

Remember that, as you think, so are you. Do not conform any longer to the patterns, traditions, and conventions of this world, but be transformed by the renewing of your mind. Trust in the Lord with all your heart and lean not unto your own understanding. In all your ways acknowledge Him, and He shall direct your path.

167

Is anything too hard for God? He wants you to be well, so He sent His Son, Christ Jesus, to take your infirmities and bear your sicknesses. Jesus tells you that it will be done to you according to your faith. He also tells you that nothing shall be impossible to you. Whatever you ask for in prayer, believe that you have received it and it will be yours.

Behold, the Lord God Almighty makes all things new. If you are a born-again believer, that means you. God knows the plans He has for you, plans to prosper you and not to harm you, plans to give you a hope and a future. Call upon Him. By His stripes you are healed. Walk in the victory of the shed blood of the Lord Jesus Christ.

O, Lord, my God, I stand on Your Word, leaving the winter of my past beliefs behind me. Every day through Your Holy Word You exhort me to choose You and to choose life. So I take hold of Your Word, Father, with a fierce determination to walk in the victory won for me by my Lord and Savior, Jesus Christ. He took the stripes for me, and He conquered the enemy for me. Every blessing of the atonement is mine – salvation, healing, deliverance, and being made whole. It's all mine because of His shed blood. Use me, Father, as a witness for Your glory and Your honor. In the precious name of Jesus, I pray, Amen.

✝

GREAT RESOURCES

Our YouTube Channel

Youtube.com/c/ProclaimingGodsWord
Be uplifted and encouraged by tranquil, inspirational videos with Scripture and music on topics such as healing, peaceful sleep, and overcoming depression.

Books and Teaching CDs

1) *Sparkling Gems from the Greek, Vol 1*
2) *Sparkling Gems from the Greek, Vol 2*
3) *Paid in Full, An In-Depth Look at the Defining Moments of Christ's Passion*
4) *A Light in Darkness*
5) *No Room for Compromise*
By Rick Renner
Renner Ministries
P.O. Box 702040, Tulsa, OK 74170-2040
918-496-3213
renner.org

1) *Dismantling Mammon*
2) *Healed: Once And For All*
3) *No More Curse*
4) *Releasing Seed That Produces Kingdom Dominion*
5) *Pressed Beyond Measure*
6) *Freedom Through the Anointing*
7) *Victory – What Would You Do If You Knew You Could Not Fail?*

By Pastor Tracy Harris
Harvest International Ministries
4000 Arkansas Boulevard
Texarkana, AR 71854
870-774-4446
experiencehim.org

1) *Authority of a Renewed Mind*
2) *Preparations for a Move of God*
3) *The Spirit of Elijah is in the Land*
4) *Hope for the Heart*
5) *Your Robe of Righteousness*
6) *Proving God*
7) *The Healing Library*

By Dr. Sandra Kennedy
Sandra Kennedy Ministries
2621 Washington Road, Augusta, GA 30904
706-737-4530
sandrakennedy.org

1) *You've Already Got It*
2) *Believer's Authority*
3) *A Better Way to Pray*
4) *The True Nature of God*
By Andrew Wommack
Andrew Wommack Ministries
P.O. Box 3333, Colorado Springs, CO   80934-3333
719-635-1111
awmi.net

1) *Atonement*
2) *You Shall Receive Power*
3) *Blessing or Curse*
4) *The Basics of Deliverance*
By Derek Prince
Derek Prince Ministries
P.O. Box 19501, Charlotte, North Carolina 28219
704-357-3556
derekprince.org

1) *The Tongue – A Creative Force*
2) *Can Your Faith Fail?*
By Charles Capps
P.O. Box 69, England, AR   72046
501-842-2576
charlescapps.org

The Living Christ in You
By James W. Gardner
P.O. Box 2127, Jasper, AL 35502
205-221-1747
jasperchristiancenter.org

Christ the Healer
By F. F. Bosworth
1973, Fleming H. Revell, division of Baker Book House Co.

How to Live and Not Die
By Norvel Hayes
Norvel Hayes Ministries
P.O. Box 1379, Cleveland, TN 37364
423-476-1018

Music – Online, Downloads, CDs

soulkeeperradio.com
Soulkeeper Radio. Streaming peaceful Christian music that will restore, renew, and refresh your soul. While you are working on your computer, have soothing Christian music playing. This is a very special website, run by Melissa and Joe Champlion.

Audiobooks
For *The Power of God's Word*

Audiobooks of *The Power of God's Word* are available at Amazon.com, iTunes.com, and Audible.com.

Books by Anne B. Buchanan

From God's Heart to Mine
This is a blank journal for recording the words that God speaks to you. There is a special foreword explaining the purpose and power of keeping this journal.
Available at Amazon.com

Christian Devotional Healing Series
If you like this book from *The Power of God's Word* Christian Devotional Healing Series, then you will love the other volumes.

Get the series:
- From Amazon.com.
- Audiobooks from Amazon.com and Audible.com.

Volume 1 – *The Power of God's Word for Healing*
70 daily devotions! You will learn:
- Why misunderstanding what the word "saved" means can keep you from being healed.
- Why saying sentences with "I am" can either help you recover or keep you sick.
- Why there is power for healing in communion.
- Why your words determine your health.
- And much more!

Volume 2 – *The Power of God's Word for Receiving Healing*

65 daily devotions! You will learn:

- Why it is critical to know the difference between facts and the truth.
- Why the unbelief of others can affect your recovery.
- How to look beyond the appearance of your ailments.
- Why not consulting God first can trap you.

Volume 3 – *The Power of God's Word for Overcoming Hindrances to Healing*

78 daily devotions! You will learn:

- Why misunderstanding Job will keep you sick.
- Why Paul's thorn was not sickness.
- Why suffering sickness does not glorify God.
- Why it is almost impossible to be healed if you don't do three important things.
- How to pray effective prayers instead of prayers that actually hinder your recovery.

Volume 4 – *The Power of God's Word for Healthy Living*

73 daily devotions! You will learn:

- Five easy habits to develop to promote your health.
- Why herbs and essential oils are God's blessings for healing.
- Three emotions that are critical for good health.
- Why it matters what music you listen to.
- Why some kinds of meditation hurt you instead of helping you.

A Final Word

I pray that you have been encouraged, lifted, and inspired by these devotions. May you walk in victory and divine health.

If you like this book, I would really appreciate your leaving a review for it at Amazon.com. It would be a blessing for me, and I would be very grateful.

End Notes

Cover photograph – "Winter Fog" by Larisa Larisa
    www.publicdomainpictures.net

Made in the USA
Monee, IL
28 October 2024

68770017R00098